SUICIDE
Vs
THE LIFE

❈ Writer ❈

Dr. Bhaskar Pundlikrao Hedaoo

M.B.B.S.

Retd. Sr. D.M.O. (I. R. M. S.)

Suicide Vs. The Life

Author's Details

Dr. Bhaskar Pundlikrao Hedaoo
M. B. B. S.
Retd. Sr. D. M. O., I. R. M. S.

Residence :
Flat No. 101, Ashwini Apartment,
Bhukum, Pune - 412115
Mob. No. 9890297595

SUICIDE Vs THE LIFE

By Dr. B. P. HEDAOO

Every Life is Precious. Life is to live and not for destruction. Life has many aspects. It's a Journey and not smooth ride. Every living has a right to lead it with self motivation. A soul is pure, as it's part of creator GOD, with all it's beauties and difficulties. Every life has it's goal to achieve as per it's capacities, abilities.

We are born to live, experience the world, accept life as it is and take efforts to live happily. Many ways and means are available on the planet. If one door shuts, other opens as dark night passes and sun rises. We are all given mind to think only human being has this asset. Every soul is different and unique. Every human life has right to be happy as per his philosophy.

Only keep your self away from **pleasure of possession, attachments** and **expectations**.

Then Happy Life is your's every bodies pleasure is different and there is no match in this world.

Don't allow anybody to influence, control your life,

Life is eternal, soul is pure, divine, mind is free and body is vehicle enjoy it.

As Lord Gautam Buddha said, "No one in this world is pure and perfect, if you avoid people to their little mistakes, you will always be alone.

So judge less and love more. If you are still looking for one, right person who will change your life, take a look in the mirror.

Happiness starts with you. Not with your relationship, your friends or your job, but with you.

Happiness or sorrow, whatever befalls you, walk on

untouched, unattached.

This ***"Suicide Vs The Life"*** is being influenced by the book, "How to stop worrying and start living authored by Dale Carnegie" Some extract from his book with my life experiences being Penned.

Dr. Bhaskar Pundlikrao Hedaoo
Retd. Sr. D. M. O. (I.R.M.S.)

INDEX

INDEX

What the 'Kota Factory' suicides say about our education system

BY INVITATION

V RAMGOPAL RAO

A series of suicide incidents in the 'Kota Factory' recently have drawn attention to the pressing issue of mental health within coaching institutions and campuses. Over the past two years alone, 38 students have taken their lives, underscoring a larger problem. While it's common to solely blame IITs and NEET/JEE exams, multiple factors have contributed to this situation. To comprehensively understand the current landscape of higher education, it's crucial to explore what led us here and potential solutions.

1. Imbalance in demand-supply ratio: With nearly a million students aspiring for engineering annually, there's a dearth of quality seats in reputable institutions. While low-quality colleges have burgeoned, institutions offering genuine quality remain scarce. Parents seek reliable career paths for their children, resulting in high demand for select institutions. Entrance exams serve as elimination tools due to the surplus of high-performing students. Coaching centres help average students prepare, turning coaching into a perceived necessity for a secure future.

2. Disparity between top and other institutions: In the US, the gap between top-tier and lower-ranked universities is narrow. Even secondary universities offer comparable undergraduate education. India's scenario differs; faculty quality and curriculum diminish significantly outside the elite institutions.

3. Media emphasis on high salaries: Sensational reporting of "one crore" salary packages fuels unrealistic expectations. Students and parents focus on cracking entrance exams to secure such lucrative salaries, despite these instances being rare. The actual median salaries at these institutions differ significantly from the hype as just about 1% of students receive such high packages.

4. Lack of resources for expansion: India lags in higher education investments. Budgetary allocation for higher education remains around 0.6-0.7% of GDP, hindering institution growth. Unlike some developed countries, India lacks a strategic approach to raise Gross Enrolment Ratio (GER) in elite institutions. Limited resources, faculty shortages, and financial constraints impede expansion. Our top institutions are dependent on the government for capital and operational expenditure making it a challenging task to support expansion.

5. Rising lower middle-class aspirations: In India, education's core purpose is often reduced to job acquisition due to the absence of guaranteed minimum living standards. The focus is on securing admissions to ensure a stable future, overshadowing passion and interests. Students and parents prioritise admissions into a good college above all else.

Addressing these issues requires:

Top-tier institution expansion: Established IITs and IISc need to become faculty-training institutions. There is an urgent need to expand on the PhD and undergraduate intake. The average PhD graduation rate per faculty in our top institutions is still below 0.5 students per year, which is low. At the current levels, what it means is, a faculty member in our top institution, on an average, produces one PhD student every two years. It needs to reach one PhD student per year per faculty at least. Investment in higher education and research is necessary to raise PhD graduation rates and maintain quality.

Study now-pay later schemes: Implementing schemes where students pay a portion of tuition during college and the rest after securing employment as a percentage of salary can ease financial pressures on institutions and government. Countries like Australia are successfully running such schemes. The loan repayment kicks in only after the student crosses a threshold income level. Because it's recovered at a fixed percentage of salary and for a fixed period of time, it also enables students to pursue diverse career interests. While the government will provide capital expenditure needed for expansion, the operational expenditure needs to be generated by the institute through such schemes.

Transparency in reporting pay packages: Institutions should be transparent in reporting salary data to prevent sensationalism and guide realistic expectations. There is a need for enforcing standardisation of the placement data reporting by institutions.

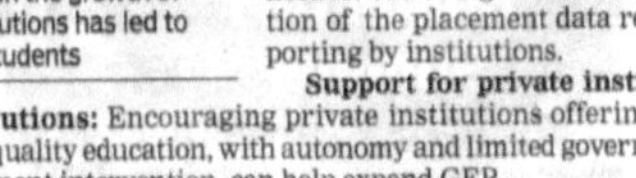

ALARM BELLS: Stagnation in the growth of quality educational institutions has led to unrealistic pressure on students

Support for private institutions: Encouraging private institutions offering quality education, with autonomy and limited government intervention, can help expand GER.

Reviving state universities: State universities have a completely different and diverse set of challenges as compared to the centrally funded institutions. It's important for NITI Aayog to initiate measures ranking states based on their support for universities. Peer pressure and a name-and-shame policy alone can resurrect them at this stage.

Implementing these measures gradually, with a focus on excellence and equity, can guide higher education toward a positive trajectory. Although reversing issues neglected for decades takes time, strategic efforts can ensure a bright future for the higher education sector. ■

Prof V Ramgopal Rao is group vice-chancellor of BITS Pilani campuses and former director of IIT Delhi. Views are personal

2nd suicide in Kota in 2 days, 18th this year

Rajiv Saxena@timesgroup.com

Kota: The country's coaching hub Kota, where many ambitious parents send their children to, is becoming the graveyard of many such dreams with recording its 18th suicide on Friday. This is second case within two days, belying local administration's claims of making all possible efforts to stop young students from ending their lives.

Bhargav Mishra, a 17-year-old engineering aspirant from Champaran district in Bihar, hanged himself from the ceiling fan in his PG room in Mahaveer Nagar area. Mishra had come to Kota in March this year for IIT-JEE coaching. According to DSP Harshraj Singh, when his parents called him up in the evening, his mobile phone was switched off. They called up the PG's caretaker, who informed police. Cops reached the spot around 8.30pm and broke the room's door. No suicide note was recovered from Mishra's room, Singh said, adding that a detailed inquiry would be initiated soon.

On Thursday, NEET aspirant Manjot Chabra from Rampur in UP had suffocated himself to death in his hostel room in Vigyan Nagar area.

Experts are alarmed over the suicides and fear that the figure could become the highest in the last nine years, if no steps are taken to prevent further such cases.

"It is shocking that despite the state having taken several measures, such as compulsory psychologists at every coaching institute, initiatives like recreational activities and weekly offs, refund policy and setting up of student helplines, the situation continues to get worse," said Puneet Sharma, an education expert.

Woman jumps into well with her 3 kids in Pathardi

Santosh.Sonawane1
@timesgroup.com

Nashik: A 30-year-old woman ended her life along with that of her three children — all below seven years — sometime between Wednesday night and Thursday morning in Malibhabul village of Pathardi taluka.

The Pathardi police have registered an FIR against the woman's husband, Dhammapal Sangade, for the offence under Section 306 of the IPC. He has been detained.

The deceased woman was identified as Kanchan Sangade (30), her son Nikhil (7) and daughters Sanchita (4) and Nishidha (2).

The police said a person from the Malibhabul village found the body of a child in a village well on Thursday morning. The villagers fished out the girl's body and started to look for her parents. They found that her mother and two siblings were also missing.

The police and villagers started drawing water from the well and the three bodies of Kanchan and her other two children were found.

The police said that on Wednesday night, Kanchan and Sangade had an argument and the woman had left.

The Pathardi police is investigating the case further.

> **A man found the body of a girl in a well. On looking for her parents, villagers realised that the mother and two siblings of the child were also missing after a fight between the parents**
>
> **Pathardi police**

Rate of suicide among men more than twice of women

1.18L Men Died By Suicide Against 45K Women In 2019-21: Study

Malathy.Iyer@timesgroup.com

Mumbai: The rate of suicide among Indian men is more than two times of that among women, shows an analysis by the International Institute for Population Sciences (IIPS), Deonar.

"Our findings show suicide rates in men were twice as compared to women in 2014, and increased to more than twice in 2021," said Dr Suryakant Yadav from IIPS, whose research paper 'Changing pattern of suicide deaths in India' was recently published in 'The Lancet Regional Health Southeast Asia'.

Suicide rate is described as the number of deaths from intentional self-harm per one lakh of population. Previously, the National Crime Records Bureau data for 2019-2021 showed that 1.18 lakh men had died by suicide as against 45,026 women.

While death by suicide has been recorded among men of all ages, the IIPS study found the majority of female victims were in the 18-29 age-group. "Low suicide among women might indicate better coping mechanisms for dealing with stress," said the paper with two supportive datapoints. Firstly, married women made up for 8.7% of the people who died by suicide as compared to men who made up for 24.3%. "Secondly, we also found that with education, the rate of suicide among women declined, but not so with men," said Dr Yadav.

However, given India's huge population, even a small percentage makes up for a big number. "Hence, despite the comparatively lower suicide rate among Indian women," Dr Yadav said, "in sheer numbers India ranks among the countries with the highest number of female suicides."

Regarding the changing patterns in suicides, the research team said a third of the victims had family issues that acted as a trigger. Economic insecurity has emerged as a big trigger too: for instance, there has been 200% rise in the suicide rate of daily wage earners from 2014 to 2021.

Interpreting the results, Dr Vibhuti Patel, former professor, Advanced Centre for Women's Studies, TISS, Deonar, said, "There is the burden of patriarchy. People are brought up in a certain way and told to be masculine. They will not take up menial jobs if they lose their respectable jobs." Women, on the other hand, are willing to take up any work or multiple jobs to keep family secure.

"During the 2008 financial crisis, many women stepped out of their homes, updated their skill-sets and took up jobs. They even didn't mind sewing or cooking after office hours to supplement family income," said Dr Patel.

Psychiatrist Dr Harish Shetty said one of the biggest changes in suicide patterns in the last few years is more teenaged girls have died than teenaged boys.

WHAT THE NUMBERS REVEAL

Year	No. of suicides	Projected population (in lakh+)	Rate of suicides
2017	1,29,887	13,091	9.9
2018	1,34,516	13,233	10.2
2019	1,39,123	13,376	10.4
2020	1,53,052	13,533.9	11.3
2021	1,64,033	13,671.8	12

Suicide victims by sex between 2019 and 2021	Men	Women	India's suicide rate of
	1,18,979	45,026	**14.04 per lakh** population in 2019 put it at 49th rank globally

To spot suicidal tendencies among students, Kota to hold psycho tests

TIMES NEWS NETWORK

Kota: With the aim to check mounting suicide cases in Kota, the district administration has decided to conduct psychological tests of every coaching students every fortnight. The test will help spot suicidal tendencies among students in time and they could be provided with timely counselling.

The decision was taken at a meeting with representatives of coaching institutes, hostels and stakeholders, held on Saturday to review the implementation of norms for coaching centres and hostels.

The evaluation of every student would be done to ascertain his/her psychological status, and those found unstable would be provided counselling by experts, district collector OP Bunker said.

At the meeting, he directed officials to ensure strict implementation of guidelines in coaching institutes, hostels and PGs.

City SP Sharad Choudhary recommended forming an association of parents whose children are studying in Kota, which would stay in touch with the district administration to share concerns of their wards. It would also ensure participation of parents in efforts to check suicide among students, he said.

Don't put pressure on kids: Gehlot

Expressing concern over the suicides, chief minister Ashok Gehlot said nearly two dozen students ending their lives in Kota in the past eight months was a "matter of grave concern for us". The CM exhorted parents not to exert pressure on their children to pursue any particular course. "Let them do what they want," he said, adding on a philosophical note that everything in life was preordained. "I am in politics by chance, but I wanted to become a doctor in my childhood. I used to study till late in the night to crack PMT, but couldn't succeed. I didn't lose hope and changed my path," he said. TNN

'Suicide is last step, watch out for warning signs'

Madhia Girotra & Shoeb Khan | TNN

The pressure of IIT coaching in Kota is too much for her, but if she quits and returns home, her mother will marry her off. Sometimes, this UP girl feels so desperate that she slashes her wrists. Experts who have studied Kota's suicide problem say this feeling of being trapped is the trigger in most cases.

Dinesh Sharma, head of the mental health department at Kota's government nursing college, recently published a paper on the risk factors for suicidal tendencies in youth. His key finding based on interviews with 400 coaching students is that academic pressure – defined as the inability to keep up with teaching in coaching institutes and schools together – is the chief cause of suicide in Kota. Family pressure comes next.

Burden Of Expectations

The UP girl seems to be crumbling under a combination of academic and family pressures. Dr M L Agarwal, a veteran psychiatrist who runs a helpline for students in Kota, has treated the girl and dozens of other stressed students. He says she is schizophrenic. "Her family knows...the medication had started in Lucknow. Yet, they dropped her here."

Such ambitious families aren't rare. Nidhi Shrivastava, a counsellor at Resonance coaching institute, remembers a parent from Kolkata who asked her, "My child will clear IIT, right? Or NIT at least?"

Pramila Shankhla, one of Agarwal's three counsellors, says, "*Har parent ka ek hi sapna reh gaya hai ki bachcha doctor ya engineer bane* (every parent wants their child to be a doctor or an engineer). Most kids are burdened with parents' expectations."

Kota superintendent of police Sharad Chowdhary also keeps turning over this question in his mind: "Why aren't parents concerned?" He says stress builds up among coaching students for various reasons: "They are away from their parents, school, friends, homemade food.... There are long study hours and no play. When they come here, their rankings get affected. Those who scored 90% in their hometown score merely 60% here."

System Multiplies Pressure

The way coaching institutes operate also combines the two pressures. Sharma's research shows the weekly test is the most stressful time for 90% of students: "The result is declared on the same day or the next day, which contributes to a change in behaviour."

But things get worse when the results are forwarded to parents. They worry why their child, who ranked in the top tier of their town, is now lagging behind, says Agarwal. The churn in rankings and the preferential treatment for star performers also affect students psychologically. "Earlier, low scorers used to be in a separate batch. Now

there are separate batches for top scorers. They are taught better in a star batch," he says.

It Gets Worse With Time

Sharma's research shows stress builds up among coaching students with time. Those who have spent less than three months in Kota are the least stressed. Whereas class 12 students who have stayed more than three months, and whose scores in weekly tests are not satisfactory, are highly strung.

But there's a class angle to this anxiety. Sharma has found that dejected students from lower- or middle-class families are more likely to commit suicide because they feel guilty about wasting scarce family resources. He says even when students realise they are not cut out for Kota, their families pressure them to continue because they have paid the tuition, hostel and mess fees in advance.

Watch Out For Signs

Kota's teaching methods won't change in a day but that does not mean student suicides are inevitable. Agarwal says, "Suicide doesn't happen all of a sudden. There are many clues before it." A student skips classes and meals, appears morose and struggles to concentrate.

Chowdhary agrees. He says the boy who committed suicide on the night of August 15 "had not been attending classes for two months... wasn't scoring well."

So, what's needed is awareness about these signs. "Faculty and hostel staff should be trained compulsorily to observe any behavioural changes in a child," says Agarwal. It would help if parents informed institutes about the mental health issues and medication of their child at the time of admission, he adds.

Nylon nets and collapsible ceiling fans are among the steps being taken by hostels to prevent suicides

'Why Didn't They Reject Her?'

On May 26, Tonk girl Sakshi Choudhary ended her life at her cousin's house in Kota. Police termed it a result of academic pressure. The 16-year-old NEET aspirant was the youngest of three sisters and had made up her mind to study in Kota two years ago. When she scored 60% in her class 10 boards this year, it was a sign that she was not cut out for studying medicine, but her father borrowed money to fulfil her wish anyway.

"We should have counselled her to join another stream," says Suresh Jat, her cousin. He's angry at her coaching institute for not turning her away after seeing her scores. "I can bet they knew she was among those thousands of students who would never clear NEET," he says.

— SHOEB KHAN

'Category System Killed My Son'

After passing out of a prestigious Prayagraj school with 75% marks in 2020, Ranjeet Singh had moved to Kanpur for coaching. Then, one and a half years later, he had decided to move to Kota against his father Ratibhan Singh's advice. "My son was good at studies and I never wanted to send him to Kota for coaching," says Ratibhan, who was shattered by Ranjeet's suicide on January 29.

Ratibhan says the coaching institute's 'category system' – based on class 12 marks and internal assessments – took a toll on Ranjeet. "My son became depressed when the institute divided students into categories. This system is driving students to depression."

Ratibhan had asked Ranjeet to return but the boy chose to stay on in Kota. "We talked normally a day before he hanged himself in his hostel room," he recalls. On January 29, Ratibhan was on a train to Kota, thinking about his son's birthday five days away. "When I arrived on January 30 morning, I found his body," he says, breaking down.

— KAPIL DIXIT

'Nobody Should Study In Kota'

Navlesh Kumar, 17, was his parents' only hope after his elder brother became bedridden with physical and mental health issues. But on May 13, the Patna boy was found hanging from the fan in his room in Kota. His uncle Sunil Kumar remembers the day he dropped Navlesh in the city. "He was a good student. Nobody forced him to go to Kota to prepare for medical entrance. We really don't know what happened there," says Sunil.

Navlesh last visited home on Holi in March. "He never mentioned any problem. There were teething troubles, but he had settled down after a month," says Sunil. All he wants now is a proper investigation into Navlesh's suicide. He's also dead set against Kota: "We would never let any other child go to Kota for preparation."

— SHEEZAN NEZAMI

Another student suicide in Kota, 3rd in 11 days and 19th this yr

Kota: Yet another teenager, preparing for IIT-JEE in Kota for the past one year, died by suicide just hours after his father left for home after spending five days with him.

Manish Prajapat (17), a class 12 student from Azamgarh in UP, hanged himself with a bedsheet from the ceiling fan in his hostel room in the city's Mahaveer Nagar area on Thursday night. This is the third suicide by a coaching student in Kota this month and the 19th this year.

Manish had dinner at the hostel and returned to his room around 7pm. His father, who was headed home by train, called him up several times. When the teen did not respond, his father asked the hostel caretaker to check on him. On peeping through the window, the caretaker found him hanging.

No suicide note was recovered from Manish's room, circle inspector at Jawahar Nagar police station, Shivraj Singh, told **TOI** on Friday. Police suspect stress might have prompted the boy to take his life, as he was reportedly weak in studies and was scoring low marks in routine tests at the institute. He was also irregular to the coaching classes.

Earlier this month, Manjot Chabra (17), a NEET aspirant from Rampur in UP, and Bhargav Mishra (17), an IIT-JEE aspirant from West Champaran in Bihar, had died by suicide last week. Manjot's parents, however, had alleged murder.

Despite the spate of suicides in Kota, a coaching hub for medical and engineering aspirants, the Rajasthan government has been mum over the Coaching Institute (Regulation and Control) Bill, raising questions about its intention to prevent such incidents. The bill, drafted by a three-member committee, was uploaded on the portal of the higher education department this year, but was not tabled in the assembly. "The reasons are obvious: strict provisions that were objected to by the multimillion-dollar coaching industry. Even the public representatives from Kota were averse to the idea of regulation," said a source. TNN

Renowned art director Nitin Desai found dead, film industry shocked

Renowned art director and production designer Nitin Chandrakant Desai reportedly died by suicide at his studio (ND Studio) in Karjat, 60 km from Mumbai, yesterday. As per reports, he was going through financial stress and speculation is that this could have been the reason for him to take this step.

In his career spanning 20 years, he worked with prominent filmmakers like Ashutosh Gowarikar, Vidhu Vinod Chopra, Rajkumar Hirani and Sanjay Leela Bhansali. He was the brain behind the sets of iconic Hindi films like *1942: A Love Story* (1994), *Hum Dil De Chuke Sanam* (1999), *Lagaan* (2001), *Devdas* (2002), *Jodhaa Akbar* (2008) and *Once Upon a Time in Mumbai* (2010), to name a few. His last venture as an art director was Ashutosh Gowariker's *Panipat* (2019). He had also created the sets for the Oscar-winning film *Slumdog Millionaire* (2008). Desai won several awards, including four National Awards.

In 2005, Desai established his ND Studio at Karjat, which was spread over 52 acres. This studio has played host to numerous movies as well as the reality show *Bigg Boss*.

Early last month, Desai had performed a *pooja* at his studio in anticipation of the upcoming festival of Ganesh Chaturthi. He was working on the *pandal* decoration for Lalbaugcha Raja's 90th celebrations. He was also busy with an OTT show on Maharana Pratap.
— With inputs from ANI

CASE UNDER INVESTIGATION

Police were informed by a worker on the set. When the police team reached the studio, we saw his body hanging. We are investigating the case further to ascertain all the aspects in this case
— Somnath Gharge, Raigad SP

FINANCIAL STRAIN TO BE BLAMED?

As per reports, Desai had defaulted on a ₹252-crore loan and a bankruptcy court had admitted an insolvency petition against his company last week.

Maharashtra MLA Mahesh Baldi also said the art director was under financial strain. "He was in deep financial trouble. I met him one or two months ago, and he spoke about the financial problems. He said the ND Studio wasn't functioning, shoots were not happening. Financial crisis was the reason why he took this step," Baldi claimed.

Sanjay Dutt
Deeply saddened to hear about the passing of Nitin Desai. A brilliant art director and a good friend, his contribution to Indian cinema has been monumental. My thoughts are with his family and friends during this difficult time

Manoj Bajpayee
So saddened and shocked to read the news of passing away of our very own NITIN DESAI! Will take some time to process this! A great artiste and lovely friend ! Why Nitin? Why? Rest in peace my friend

Ketan Mehta
We have worked on many films together like *Mangal Pandey: The Rising* (2005) and *Rang Rasiya* (2014). He was an incredibly talented art director and production designer. Hailing from a humble background, he managed to come a long way. He has done some incredible work with a wide range of filmmakers. It is difficult to believe the news because he was such a spirited man. His sudden demise has shocked me

Madhur Bhandarkar
Just heard the devastating news about the passing of multiple National award-winning Art Director Nitin Desai. It's hard to believe. I had the privilege of working with him on four remarkable films — *Traffic Signal*, *Fashion*, *Jail* and *Indu Sarkar*. His immense talent and extrovert personality made every project unforgettable. Indian cinema has lost a true gem. Heartfelt condolences to his family members. We will miss you, Dada

Too Few Seats For The Kotas

Parents, governments, recruiters and teachers must recognise there are too few professional colleges for too many student aspirants. Broken dreams are inevitable

Chetan Bhagat

The news of more student suicides in Kota should worry us greatly about the increasing numbers of such deaths countrywide. Kota gets disproportionate attention because at any point lakhs of students are grinding away in its coaching classes. They hope to crack the hyper-competitive medical and engineering entrance exams, which according to many Indian parents are the safest if not the only possible careers.

The coaching classes are expensive, which places a heavy burden on many parents. The students are aware of what the parents are doing for them, creating stress right from Day One. Staying away from home is tough too. The coaching is intense. Cracking these exams with minuscule selection rates, reportedly 2% isn't a cakewalk. The stress comes to a boil with the entrance exam results. A selection rate of 2% means 98% of students will not make it. Are you really surprised that some of the students just crumble in this journey?

People have suggested solutions, from spring-loaded fans (to prevent death by hanging) to more counsellors. But to fully solve the problem we need to first have the courage to see the reality.

We must realise this is not just a Kota phenomenon. In 2019, 7.4% of all deaths by suicides were of students. According to NCRB, over 13,000 teens died by suicide in India in 2020 alone: that made it 34 students taking their own lives each day across the country. Kota is estimated to have around two lakh students registered in various coaching institutes. Till August 28, 23 students in this coaching town died by suicide - six reported in August alone. This is an alarming statistic. However, student stress and suicides are a national issue.

The question is, what can we really do to fix it? There's a role for everyone – parents, teachers, policy makers, job recruiters and the students themselves.

● Indian parents, for heaven's sake, please educate yourselves. Please stop imposing your dreams on your children. Being a doctor or engineer is not the be all and end all of life. There are literally hundreds of other professions. Most doctors in India don't even make so much money. Many engineers are unemployed.

Have you ever heard of industries like real estate and finance? People in these industries can become really wealthy. A shopkeeper, social media marketing executive, car dealer, hotelier, travel industry expert, online store owner – all these people DO NOT have to be doctors and engineers. Nobody who works in the newspaper publishing this article needs to be a doctor or engineer. They also live happy lives. They also get 'rishtas'.

● Teachers, you must realise how dumb and pig-headed Indian parents can be. You have to re-educate the students on how to approach these exams, not just on how to study for them. The exams are to-

Show the world that you don't need to be another boring engineer or doctor to make your mark in it. This is what will make this doctor-engineer-entrance-exam tyranny end. Do it for you, and for the students who come after you

-ugh and they must work hard. But treat it like a challenging game. If it happens, great. If it doesn't, move on. Life has something better in store.

● Policy makers, you need to see why even now only a few government colleges are considered aspirational. This when people in India otherwise prefer their products and services private. It's because private colleges have got poor credibility and their motives are not trusted. Maybe let foreign universities come in? Maybe make big Indian corporate houses affiliate with colleges? We need to increase the supply of aspirational colleges and seats.

● Indian recruiters, if you only go to elite colleges to recruit only engineers, you are not helping. Why do you need a mechanical engineer for a sales job? Why not go to other, less elite colleges and pick good students from there?

● Students, learn this bitter truth about life that life is unfair, uphill and hard. People may dole out lip-service on how student stress should be lowered but nobody is coming to save you. However, the good thing is it is up to you to make your own life. Life will hit you with disasters, as it does everyone. A failure in an entrance exam may be a blow and a dream shattered but see this as practice for what's to come. Failure, disappointment, and unfairness will come to you again and again. The answer to this is not to quit on life, but to change your goals, strategy and actions.

Continue to hustle and work hard but in a different direction. Do not think that all those years of grinding for an exam went to waste as you didn't clear it. The hard work you did will prepare you for life. Life may have taken away an opportunity from you today, but in the long life ahead, more opportunities will come. You may be at rock-bottom today but the only way is up.

Do not take an extreme step. Just breathe. Take a break, rise up again and come to fight back stronger. Show the world that you don't need to be another boring engineer or doctor to make your mark in it. This is what will make this doctor-engineer-entrance-exam tyranny end. Do it for you, and for the students who come after you.

No student deserves to reach a point when they abandon hope. This isn't about Kota, this is about us. This isn't about a child failing at an entrance exam and quitting on life. It is about us failing as a society and quitting on our responsibility to show our children a better future.

1. Suicide : A Global Menance

Whenever I go through News paper, I encounter news regarding suicides, which are alarmingly increased from last 5 decades; due to causes which are trivial; genuine, and untreatable in very few cases.

These are the personalities who are quite emotional and impulsive, which takes such drastic steps to end life. This may be gradually developed; or suddenly triggered impulsive action to cause catastrop.

Any thing which hurts self esteem leading to disinterest in life, frustration, unworthiness, considering him / her self <u>unwanted, lonely and unsupported</u>.

This type of disinterest in life leads to suicidal tendency drip by drip in mind. Due to lack of openness lack of faith, they do not interact with anybody and hence could not receive sympathetic support and required help.

There can be many causes to develop suicidal tendency, known, but sometimes unknown.

I have tried to enumerate causes as follows, which I feel one of them acts as trigger for this menance.

Causes :-

1. Emotional blow to self-esteem
2. Hurt by family members constantly
3. Betrayal of Dear one
4. Domestic Violence
5. Extra Marital Affairs
6. Poverty - Financial Distress
7. Sudden Loses in Business
8. Failure of self made plans and decisions

9. Educational stress and strains

10. Inferiority Complex

11. Failure of Love affair, Love Breakages

12. Family Wreckage

13. Unemployment

14. Sexual dissatisfaction / desires

15. Lack of faith inself and others

16. Feeling of Loneliness

17. Maladjustment with realities

18. Inability to cope with situation which leads to constant pressure worries at place of employment

19. High expectation of families , inability to fullfill even after much struggle and efforts, causing distress, anxiety, despair

20. Inability to fullfill Self Desires and Expectation, may be due to non-availability of resources or over expectation beyond capacity to cause despair, depression.

21. Constant resentment over trivial causes

22. Personal emotional wreckage due to ill health, chronic illness, unbearable bodily painful conditions, Neurological disorders

23. Molestation / Rapes

24. Addiction

25. Low resistant power for adjustment with situation - Leading to frustration, personality disorders, unknown fears Anxiety, Pessimism

26. Feeling of Insecurity

27. Loss of self image and it's feeling

28. Lack of Flexibility of mind / fix, stiff minds

29. Negativism - Negative approaches to each and every thing

And many more can be there, known or unknown.

I have tried to understand, which I could understand as above.

Common Methods adopted for Suicide

Easy available self destructive

1. Weapons : Razor, Blades, knife in home some times firearms.

2. Poisoning

3. Hanging

4. Jumping from High rise buildings

5. Fire

6. Drowning

7. Road / Rail track suicides

Especially in India Firearms are 'difficult to be available, like in USA firearms are easily available.

As per WHO

On an average, some one commits suicide in United State of America, Every 30 minutes and some one goes insane every 120 minutes.

Most of these suicides and insanity tragedies could have been prevented if these people had solace and peace, that are found in religion and prayer.

As per report from Geneva, one million people kill themselves each year number which exceeds death toll from murder and wars, which is expected to hit 1.5 million by 2020 Times of India, Pune dated 10/09/2004.

Suicide is a tragic Global Public Health Problem said Catherine Le Eales, WHO the then, Assistant Director General for non-commuicable and Mental Health.

Worldwide more people die from suicide than from Homicide, wars combined. So there is an urgent need for co-ordiated and intensified Global Action to prevent the needless death toll.

Many more men and women take their lives, But greater number of women attempt suicide. WHO estimated, noteing that 10-20 millions try to commit, but fail to kill themselves annually.

Among the countries that report suicide deaths. The highest suicidal rate are found in Eastern Europe, Lowest in Latin America; The Muslim nation and Asian states according to Geneva based WHO data.

Rate of suicide tends to increase with age. But there has been alarming increase in suicidal behaviour among young population aged between 15-25 years as per reports given by WHO.

Suicidal behaviour has a large number of complex underlying causes as a whole, but few important like poverty, unemployment, Broken Relationship, Domestic Violence, Loss of near and Dear ones, Molestations and Rapes, Legal and work related problems sudden losses in Business.

In a bid to raise awareness on issue WHO And International Association for suicide prevention had hold 2nd Annual World Wide Suicide prevention day on Friday 10.09.2004.

But since then also suicides neither controlled nor prevented and more and more cases reported. That shows steps taken are insufficient to prevent this global public health problem.

Statistical Data

In Countries - South Africa, Eastern Europe - Annual 15 death / Lac last 20 years.

In Europe, South America, Asia - 10 death / Lac Annually last 20 years.

As per book by Saloni Dattani Lucas Rodes

According to NIHM (National Institute of Health)

The Total Rate adjusted - Suicide Rate in U.S. increased by 35.2% i.e. from 10.4 / Lac in 2000 to 14.2 / Lac in 2020.

In India 1,64033 in 2021 i.e. 12 death /Lac Highest since 1967 as per Peeter Varnik from WHO Geneva.

China, Russia, Japan, South Korea are biggest contributor to absolute number adjusted Annually is 10.5/Lac while as a whole world i.e. 11.6/Lac.

In India in last 50 years rising trend observed.

In 2021 suicide rate increase by 7.2% compared 2020. It increased from 25.3% in 1990 to 36.6 in 2016 among female population.

In male population from 18.7 in 1990 to 24.3% in 2016.

Daily Wages Earner registered - 42004 death in 2021 biggest group in suicide data.

In 2021Maharashtra state recorded 22207 death by suicide.

Tamil Nadu (T.N.) - 18925

Madhya Pradesh (M. P.) - 14965

West Bengal (W. B.) - 13500

Karnatak State - 13506

Male : Female Ratio 72.5 : 27.4

Estimated number varies in study presented in Lancet 1,87,000 in 2016 while Government of India, Dada claims 1,34,600 in 2016.

Similarly for 2019 NRCB reported 10.4/Lac. But while WHO in 2019 shows 12.9/Lac.

Male - 14.7/Lac

Female - 11.1/Lac

Above data and reports, makes very clear, that most complex psychological aspects are at the root of the suicide, which are to be stressed and be tackled through concrete efforts. Mental and moral support can only be helpful than any other means.

Major causes like depression fear, insecurity, envy, frustration, maladjustment of environment, they are unable to cope with situation arised. Even more modern amenities since developed through science for comfortable living are not sufficient to mental peace.

The young community between 15-25 years of age are more inclining to suicidal tendencies.

If studied well the causes can be found, if timely taken care of may prevent many such deaths.

Mostly in young generation causes are

1.	Stress and strain of Education; family expectation from childhood

2.	Insecurity feeling

3.	Fear of competition in educational institutions, admissions, fear of Laggind behind

4.	Love relationship - sexual desires and cap on it due to moral values in communities

5.	Family opposition for love relationship

6. Arguments with family members
7. Broken love affairs
8. One sided love inclination
9. Parental disturbance
10. Regular quarrel between parents
11. Parents Divorces
12. Lack of understanding of age related requirements; and close atmosphere in society
13. Lack of Guidance of psychological needs
14. Sexual assaults and molestation and guilt feeling there off
15. Unemployment

In aged group above 30 years

1. Unsatisfactory family life
2. Lack of faith and mutual understanding
3. Employment related stress
4. In sufficient earning resources greater family expectation and non-cooperation of family members
5. Distrust - between spouses - misunderstanding, loss of love, lack of love bonds.
6. Extra marital affairs out of dissatisfied relationship
7. Loss (Death) of one of the life partner
8. Broken trust one of the spouse
9. Doubtful nature
10. Sudden financial crisis, like loss of job, business losses unbalanced expenditures and loan
11. Illness - Chronic Diseases
12. Painful Body condition

13.   Neurological Diseases

14.   Dependency on family members

All above causes leads to insecurity, anxiety, depression, despair frustration, hopelessness, unwanted feeling, loneliness translating into suicidal tendency and ultimately attempt to suicide - suicidal death, if not properly, timely intervened.

So to preserve precious lives, more vigilant eye have to be kept. Timely counseling sympathetic approach will be helpful.

As already mentioned most of causes which seems difficult to overcome in the eyes and minds of person going through such situation are preventable if intervened on early warning signs, timely action taken can very well be fruitful.

Till now, I have tried to enumerate possible causes. Now we will see about preventable aspects to avert further loss of life.

ಬಜಬ●ೞೞ

2. Preventive Aspects

1. Understanding the exact cause in a manner that will create trust between the person in distress / dispair and who may be friend, relative, doctor, spiritual adviser who so ever be.

2. Developing interest in beautiful world created by almighty God. Making him/her understand life is just beautiful to live. Once given to be lived joyfully.

3. Improving self confidence through modern techniques.

4. Keeping vigil on activities and showing concern through sympathetic approach.

5. Taking interest in them.

6. Restricting availability of self destructive equipments, like weapon, poisons ropes, fire, keep away from water bodies preventing rail/road approach. High rise building accompanying to avoid loneliness. Keeping them busy in some or other work, so as to keep away from self destructive thoughts.

Thus keeping vigilant eye, keeping busy, preventing loneliness, boosting self confidence, inculcating self interest, further educating, training how to overcome worries, situation. How to face and adjust environment, psychological treatment, counseling and further psychiatrist consultation.

Emphasizing in mind that, creater has created the world with all it's beauties and resources for every living being including human and animal kingdom on the planet, where we are. Energy sources like sun, ever lasting energy source; Air / O2 and water for every life on the earth including human and animal kingdom. Creator expects from his creations that they should enjoy his resources as per need and remain happy and joyous.

He has created opportunities for every living being to fulfill desires and their needs.

So everybody should respect to the creator, Parents who had taken care of them from first day of life, tried to arrange for every need, fulfill all requirements to grow them up. They had taken much pains, as from birth, mother has tolerated labour pain, feed them with breast milk, gave them every support to bring them up to their own feet and develop opportunities through education to live life as you desire.

Life is to live and not for destruction. There are always two sides of life bright and dark as days and nights both must be understood, experience the down fall and climb up of the life and enjoy charm of life; as successful mountaineers.

ಐಐಐ●ಐಐ

3. Treatment

In most of cases, warning signs are present, if carefully watched and observed.

1. Once detected suicidal tendency keep subject under strict vigil.

2. He / She must not be allowed alone.

3. Support role of family and friends is very important to avert untoward.

4. Extraction of possible cause with sympathetic approach.

5. Supporting through boosting mental attitude.

6. Encouraging subject to express hidden fears.

7. Developing interest in life.

8. Keeping busy in some or other work and thus no time be left for worries.

9. Remove loneliness and feeling of it through friends, family members, relative showing sincere concern.

10. Sow the ideas of possible realities of life. Good and bad experiences, occurs in every bodies life. Emphasizing every problem may have some solution, under the sun, through proper understanding and guidance.

11. Role of voluntary organization.

12. Help through psychologist and psychiatric assessments.

Only and effective ways of tackling most of these problems are

1. Religion newer concept

2. Knowledge and techniques of How to abate worries.

3. Self control over situation in odd times.

4. Removing self centered thoughts

5.   Making and realizing to understand life is precious and once got, to be preserved at any cost and lived fully.

6.   GOD created human race along with colourful world with diversities, which are worthy for living with satisfied mind. Lot of opportunities are available for every one to full fill their desires and achievements.

Inculcating in mind of subject, that peace and happiness is within the innerself. It cannot be bought or served. The wrong notions, need to be removed, unless such negative thought replaced by positive thoughts, you will not be able to create interest in life. Once pessimism is over, we will be able to decrease suicidal tendencies.

Only surveillance will not be fruitful, they may find another alternate to get through. The principal need is change in "Perception of Life". Change of thought processing is very essential and integral part of the change of mind.

One of my professor of English Mr. Panse, when I was studying in V. M. V. College, Amaravati, he very often use to say "Time is the best solution of each and every problem. Let the time pass, problem will be solved." Very small, but great advise.

Desires have no limits, it is very much necessary to differentiate between need, wants and greed. Remain contented, keep your needs under control.

There was report few years back that only few people i.e. 30 Billionaires control the wealth of half the population of the world that means only 30 Billionaires have such amaze wealth of 1/2 of the planet population. Such vast difference in distribution of wealth is there. It does not mean, these handful of Billionaires are grabbing, but they are very much struggling for better world to live for rest of human race. They are developing science and technology to that extend to be available for whole human population of the planet.

Even then some greed is behind that, competition between big sharks as human nature is like that, "Every human desires to be great." Which is one of the important ingredient of development of this world. Many of these wealth creaters are turning to philanthropy and vast donation are given by them to the needy countries for betterment and advancement of their population. Super rich like 'Billgate', Asim Premji, TATA's, Ambani's there is long list of such super rich, who are trying to uplift some poor population. But even then, it is necessary to achieve fair distribution of resources available on the planet.

So far as financial problem, mind should be focused on need, requirements change of earning methods, with in our capacity our resources.

Family co-operaction is very much essential to come out of situation from financial crisis rather than ridiculing the earning member for deficiencies.

Betrayal can be managed through mutual understanding and removing of underlying causes and misunderstanding, through open discussions and counseling with psychological support, a marathi proverb, ''एखाद्याचे विष ते दुसऱ्याचे अमृत'' that means something is poisonous for one may be amrut for other one; that is different views are for different personalities we have to consider others view with his angle.

Foundation of life, building process should start from school level, students along with knowledge should also be made aware of odd and even of life situations, emphasizing in mind they are tender and easily accepting advises, regarding beautiful world, full of happiness for grate living as well some dark spots of situation may arise during living, there are struggles in life in achievement they also may be made aware of hills and valleys while climbing the mountain of desires and own interest.

Even parents should also understand that, they should not try to serve their children ready made happiness in plates. They must be taught from tender ages that nothing without effort will be achieved in life. As Buddha said, "You don't find happy life, you make it." A very good book I read, "Rich Dad, Poor Dad", the author had very well narrated how to bring up your kids, to make them strong to fight in life.

They must be made aware of "Your comfort zone will destroy, your dreams" so they have to come out of comfort zone many times, to fulfill their desires. "Hardship often prepares an ordinary person for an extraordinary destiny."

"Without rain nothing grows; learn to embrance the storm of your life", "We fall, we brake, we fail, but then we rise, we heal, we overcome." Have patience; all thing are difficult before they become easy. Big dreams require healthy habits and healthy habits requires self discipline. So they are to be prepared for struggle with fighting spirit with odds in life.

Dr. Carl Jung most distinguished psychiatrist in his book penned, "Modern man in search of soul."

He said, "During last 30 years people from all the civilized countries on the earth consulted me. I have treated many hundreds of patients, among all my patients in the second half of life i.e. say above 35 years. There had not been one, whose problem in the last resort was not that finding a religion, and religious out look on life."

"It is safe to say that everyone of them fall ill because he had lost, living religious." Religion over every age have given to their followers and none of them has been really reacted; who did not regain his religious out look."

William James said, "Faith is one of the forces which human race lives and total absences of it means collapse."

Mahatma Gandhi said, "Without prayer I should have been lunatic long ago."

When we are harrashed and reached the limit of our own strength many of us then turn in desperation to GOD. Then, why to wait for desperation? Why not renew our strength everyday.

Prayer has tremendous power, will energize your nerves to courage and give spirit to face any sort of bad situation. It creates fighting with evil forces which are encircling your mind, and how to conquer and come out of your bad positions.

Dr. Alexis Carleel, Nobel prize winner said, "Prayer is the most powerful form of energy, one can generate. It is force as true as terrestrials gravity." He further said, "I have seen men after all other therapies had failed; lifted out of diseases and melancholy by serene effect in prayer.

Prayer like radium is a source of luminous, self generating energy. In prayer human being seek to arrangements their infinite energy by addressing themselves to infinite source of energy.

When we pray, we link ourselves with the inexhaustible motive power that spins the universe. We pray that a part of this power to operation to our needs. Even in asking our human deficiencies are filled and we arouse, strengthened and repaired. When ever we address GOD in fervent prayer we charge both our body, mind and soul for better happening. Our full faith on almighty wipes out our negativity and energize us for better outcome. It could not happen that any man or woman pray for single moment, come out without good result. This is a power of prayer and faith.

Richer Byra (Admiral) when in captivity for 5 months, has been alone wrote in his diary, "I am not Alone." He added few men in their lifetime come anywhere near, exhausting resources dwelling within them. There are deep wells of strength; that never used. Richer Byra learned to tap those wells of strengths and use those resources by turning to GOD through prayer.

Glenn A. Arnold said, "As I look back, I am glad now that, I lost everything and became so depressed that I started for river, because this tragedy taught me to rely on GOD and now, I have peace and confidence, that I never dreamt were possible."

Why does spiritual faith bring as such peace and calm, fortitude? William James answered it. He said, "The turbulent billows of fretful surface leave the deep parts of the ocean undisturbed, and to him has a hold on water and more permanent realities, the hourly vicissitudes of his personal destiny seems relatively significant things."

The truly religious and spiritual person with faith is accordingly unshakable and full of equanimity and calm, ready for any duty that the day may bring forth.

Even if you are not religious by nature or training, even then you are out and out skeptic. Prayer can help you much more than you believe, for it is practical thing. What do I mean 'Practical'?

"Prayers full fills their basic, psychological need, which all people share, whether they believe in GOD or not."

Prayers help us to put into words exactly, what is troubling you. As we saw, it is almost impossible to deal with problem, while it remains vague and nebulous. Prayer is a way very much like writing our problems down on paper. That means if you ask help for our problem even from GOD, we must put it into clear words. Problem well stated is half solved.

Words are keys, if you choose them right, they can open any heart and shut any mouth.

Prayer gives us sense of sharing our burden, as not being alone. Few of us are so strong that we can bear our heaviest burden, our most agonizing troubles all by ourselves. Sometimes our worries are of such nature that we cannot discuss them, even with our closest friends and relatives; Then prayer is the only answer.

Any psychiatrist will tell us that, when we are pent up and tense, in agony of spirit. It is therapeutically good to tell someone, share your feelings, problems troubles with someone, you believe, if that's not possible for any reason. It is very possible to tell GOD through prayer.

Prayer puts into force an active principal of 'Doing'. It is first step towards action.

I doubt if anyone play for some fulfillment day after day without benefitting from it, in other words it is impossible without stepping out to bring it pass.

Prayer is most powerful form of energy one can generate so why not to make use of it.

You may call it GOD, Bhagwan, Allah, spirit, what ever it may be. There is no reason to quarrel with defination and designation as long as mysterious power house of nature takes us in hands.

The beautiful prayer written by Saint Francis of Assis 700 years back.

Prayer

Lord make me an instrument of the Peace.

Where there is hatred, Let me sow love.

Where there is injury - Pardon

Where there is doubt - Faith

Where there is despair - Hope

Where there is darkness - Light

Where there is sadness - Joy

'O' Divine Master grant that

I may not so much seek to be

consoled as to console

To be understood, as to understand

To be loved as to Love

For it is giving, that we receive

It is pardoning, that we are pardoned

And It is in dyeing, that we are born to Eternal Life.

Here I also remember the Prayer in Hindi

इतनी शक्ती हमें देना दाता,

मन का विश्वास कमजोर हो ना ।

हम चले नेक रस्ते पे हमसे,

भूलकर भी कोई भूल हो ना ।

दूर अज्ञान के हो अंधेरे,

तू हमें ज्ञानकी रोशनी दे ।

हर बुराई से बचते रहे हम,

जितनी भी दे, भली जिंदगी दे ।

बैर होना किसी का किसी से,

भावना मनमें बदले की हो ना ।

हम चले नेक रस्ते पे,

भूलकर भी कोई भूल हो ना ।

हम ना सोचे, हमें क्या मिला है ।

हम ये सोचे, किया क्या है अर्पण ।

फूल खुशीयोंके बाँटे सभी को

सबका जीवन ही बनजाएँ मधुबन

अपनी करूणा का जल तू बहाॅके

कर दे पावन हर एक मनका कोना ।

हम चले नेक रस्ते पे हमसे

भूलकर भी कोई भूल होना ।

My own prayer, in my life, which I pray.

हे परमपिता, परमात्मा, परमशक्ती

हे ब्रह्मांड के रचेयता, पालनकर्ता, संहारक

आप चराचरमें चैतन्यरूपसे व्याप्त है

आप हर जीव में, आत्मारूपसे निवास करते है

हे प्रभु, आपकी इच्छासेही सृष्टी प्रकाशीत है

आपकी इच्छासे ही सृष्टी चक्र चलायमान है

आपकी इच्छासे सृष्टी को गती प्राप्त है

आपकी इच्छाके बिना एक पत्ता भी नहीं हिलता

हे परमपिता, मुझे ज्ञान एवं दृष्टी प्रदान करे

मैं आपके आशीष से किसीकी सेवा कर सकू

आपकी महिमा को समझकर जीवन के सार को पा सकू

हे ईश्वर, मझे शक्ती प्रदान करे, शक्ती प्रदान करे ।

Till now we have gone through the problems, causes, preventive measures and suggested remedies which a person may encounter in life. Now further we will find solutions. How to abate worries, difficult situation to come out through it safely and successfully. We will learn to live life to full extent, Happily and purposefully.

4. Never Allow Anybody to Hurt Your self esteem

Never Compromise self Respect"

During my carrier as medical officer in Railways in 1990, When I was working at Khadwa (M. P.). I faced a situation when my senior Dr. I will not name him here, as I don't want to expose his identity.

His attitude was far from tolerable. He was not doing his duties properly and expecting all duties from me. I was doing all train calls colony calls from railway Pts. 24 x 7 even then, he was just to satisfy his ego, wanted to keep control on me of his seniority, misbehaved with me which in turn hurt my self-esteem, and hence I decided to teach him a lesson, in place of succumbing to his selfish attitude.

I decided to resign from my post and forwarded my 3 months notice of resignation to CMD Central Railway, Mumbai, who was competent authority for acceptance of resignation.

As soon as I served the notice I decided to shift myself from working place. I vacated Railway Quarter, shifted my family to Nagpur immediately and after applying leaves for few days shifted to Nagpur. I planed to start my medical practice there.

I remained almost 1 year out of my job, but railway had not accepted my resignation.

During that period I explained, the then C.M.D. Dr. V. D. Mathur in which situation I had to decide such drastic action.

Dr. V. D. Mathur C.M.D. who was very well known administrator and very kind officer, on his investigation, he refused to accept my resignation.

He then transferred Sr. Doctor from Khandwa and then, I was asked why I am not taking back my resignation and join.

I was called then to C.M.D. office Mumbai. When I met C.M.D. in his office he put same question, why I am not joining. I replied him Sir, I was not wrong, that fellow was just tries to satisfy his ego was harassing me, so I will not take back my resignation but if you consider me and call me with dignity I will join.

After few days, I received Letter from Personal Branch Central Railway, Mumbai stating; "Your resignation has not been agreed by competent authority and hence advised to join with in the period 1 month."

Then I joined immediately. I had not compromised myself esteem.

Never allow anybody to hurt your self-esteem to keep image intact in your own eyes. "Never compromise self-esteem."

5. Live In Water tight Compartment

Thomas Carlyle "Our main business is not to see, what lies dimly at a distance but to do what lies clearly at hand."

Shut off the past, Let the dead past, bury it, as it is dead, It will never come back again. Past has already gone, do not look back to it, remove buried memories from your mind, which are not of any use.

"Your past is a place to learn and grow not a place to live."

The load of tomorrow, added to that of yesterday, carried today makes stringent flatter.

So shut the future as tightly as past you have today, there is no tomorrow. The day of man's salvation today and now. Be thankful for today because in one moment, your entire life could change.

Waste of energy, mental distress nervous worries do step in a man, who is anxious about future.

Dr. Sir William Osler, does not mean do not take effort to prepare for tomorrow. He means best possible way to prepare for tomorrow is to concentrate with all your intelligence, ability, enthusiasm on doing today's work superbly today, which will decide your tomorrow; and it is the only possible way to prepare for tomorrow.

Jesus Mole accurately said, "Have no anxiety for tomorrow."

In the film 3 Idiots, while advising to his friend Raju Rancho (Amir Khan) said, "You are fearful of your future. If you afraid of your future so much, how will you face, tackle your future. He advised him to be bold and prepare for tomorrow and live worriless.

This means careful thought and planning and preparation without having anxiety and fear and worries, for tomorrow.

That is clear from above version, plan your today, with sincerely doing your job at hand with almost with your capacity and capability, complete it with best of your ability, that will decide you future.

The main difference in good thinking and bad thinking is this.

"Good thinking deals with causes and effects leads to logical constructive planning, Bad thinking leads to tension, nervous worries."

ಬಬ●ಚಚ

6. HOUR-GLASS EFFECT

As Hourglass can pass, one grain of sand at one time, some way try to accomplish one prime task at one time, and leave other for some other time. That means at one time, the task at hand to be accomplished through proper planning and with all efforts to be put to make it superb and excellent, which will work as foundation of your future.

Robert Louis Stevenson wrote "Any one can carry his burden however hard for a day." Any one can live sweetly, patiently, lovingly, purely till the sun goes down. This is all the life really mean.

"Everyday is a new life to a wise-man." Horace Roman poet wrote thirty years before Christ.

"Happy the man and happy he alone
He who calls today his own
He who secure with in can say
Tomorrow do the worst for
I have lived today."

Most tragic thing of human nature is that "All of us tend to put off living."

We all dream for some magical roses garden over the horizon; instead on enjoying roses that are blooming outside of our windows today. Life we learn too late living, is in living in the tissue of every date and hour. The Rule is as white queen said, "Jam tomorrow, Jam yesterday, but never Jam today."

Dante said, "Think this day will never dawn again."

Today is our most sure possession i.e. philosophy of Lowell Thomas.

This is the day, which the lord that hath made, We will rejoice and be glad in it." wrote Jaon Ruskin on his desk on stone carved a ward, "Today".

From above great philosophers had tried to advise, all in all today is a day to live in full length and breadth."

J. P. Waswani, "In this world of transience only the present moment belongs to you, the moment that is just over in no longer yours. The moment to come may not belongs to you at all, therefore realize the worth of present moment."

Think this is the last day of life and live it fully all moments should be peaceful, joyous and happy.

Kalidas Indian dramatist's poem

"Salvation to the DAWN"
Look to this day, for it is life
The very life of life
In it's brief cause
Lie all the varieties and realities of your existance
The bliss of growth
The glory of action
The splender of beauty
For yesterday is but a dream
And tomorrow is only a vision
But today well lived, makes every yesterday
address of happiness
Such a salvation to the DAWN
The whole idea is living in today,
make it best as much as can
As it will never comeback once gone.
So the Rule is "Live in water tight compartment"

7. FORMULA FOR ANTI WORRYING TECHNIQUE

Mr. Willis H. Carrier

Step :-

1. Analyse situation fearlessly and honestly, figure out worst, that could happen as a result of failure.

2. Accept the worst possible situation if necessary.

3. Calmly devote time and energy to improve upon the worst, which is mentally accepted.

So instead of worrying think of the problem, concentrate on concrete solution to solve it logically, with applying total mind and intelligence.

As only worrying, loose power of decision making. Once you accept the worst possible mentally and made yourself ready to face it, then act immediately.

This technique is quite valuable practical, which can raise you from clouds of thoughts and worries.

Here I would like to narrate my own story as an example, when I had to adopt this technique in my life.

In 2000, when I was working as Sr. D.M.O. Central Railway at Wardha, Maharashtra state. I had to face a critical situation, Due to family pressure to have a house for which, I was not prepared and was not in position to plan even.

But to fulfill the desire of family, I had to make decision to purchase a house. I had withdrawn Rs. 3,00,000/- from my Provident Fund for down payment requirement and further amount to be taken as loan from HDFC. We then planned to purchase of duplex of 4 bed rooms in Bhopal, which was at that time in good locality and gated colony by Minal Residency. We had visited the Builder paid him down payment with Bank Draft which was arranged from P. F. withdrawal.

The builder had connection with House Loan providers and they arranged further loan of 5,50,000/- from HDFC.

Thus the purchase was finalized. Their monthly E.M.I. payment was to be paid through my salary, when calculated it comes around 11,000/- per month.

At that time, I was drawing salary of Rs. 28,000/- per month after I. T. deductions apart from this additional E.M.I. previous loan payment were also due

1. For computer for elder daughter for B. E. Computer Science.

2. For Two Wheeler for my 2nd daughter who had just cleared 10th std. was in need of vehicle for school and tuition classes.

So expenditure was heavy

Income Salary Loan Payments

Income	**Expenditure**
Rs. 28,000/- P. M	Computer Rs. 3,000/- P.M.
	Scooty (Two wheeler) Rs. 3,000/- P.M.
	Housing Loan Rs. 11,000/- P.M.
	Elder daughter Graduation Rs. 7,000/- P.M.
	Total Net Out Go 24,000/- P.M.
	Domestic Monthly Expenses +V

Expenditure against Salary of Rs. 28,000/-

Now 2nd daughter 11th std. school & Tuition and son in 8th std. school expenses were to born, with family expenses. Domestic / Home expenses, which were very well crossing the budget to deficit, which I could sustain 3 years with situation unknown to family members.

They were not made aware of financial crisis, as I was running out deficit budgetary sustainability.

In 2003, I was going to complete 20 years of my service and preparing in my mind for voluntary retirement. As, my elder daughter was in 3rd year of her graduation, 2nd daughter will be completing 12th std. and son will be completing 10th std. in March / April 2004 and all three children coming to higher education.

There was huge gap between income and expenses and further eminent expenses of higher education of two more kids.

In the month of August 2003, I had a talk with my wife regarding financial situation and eminent expenses.

I tried her to convince about my plan of Voluntary Retirement and how can I manage future expenses. But as was expected the idea of losing job to manage situation was not approved / accepted by family.

But I was very much convinced in my mind that my plan will workout. Hence, I started to execute my plan, by serving notice for 3 month, i.e. October 2003 to December 2003. According to my calculation if I go for Voluntary Retirement, I will receive around 12,00,000/- (Twelve Lakhs) of balanced fund and Rs. 7,500/- Pension P. M.

I served notice on 1st October 2003 with request to relieve me on 31st December 2003.

There was tremendous pressure from all side family pressure, pressure from relatives even from department officers, as nobody was supporting to my idea.

But as I had made my mind after careful study of my situation. Facts and preparation my mind to face worst if failed. That was a calculated risk which I had taken, rather surgical decision.

Now hurdle was from C.M.D. accepting authority. He tried to convince me to reconsider my action.

Then I was called at Mumbai by C.M.D. Dr. Parmar the then HOD and competent authority for accepting Voluntary Retirement. I went prepared with all facts.

I, explained to Dr. Parmar C.M.D. in words, as follows -

Sir, Everybodies perception is like this, I have a good job, decent salary also, they are right also. In other words as a Railway Officer, I have free Railway Travel Pass, with reservation in AC II and proceeding with family to a resort to avail vacation, I am waiting for train on platform for coming trian to board it for travel, this was every bodies perception.

But I know, I have reservation. A free pass for travel, train is going to enter in station, but I am in between the track if I remain standing, I will get run over and crushed. So I have to jump out of track, which is a only way to save myself, this is my perception and factual situation. There is no choice. This explanation convinced my C.M.D. and he agreed for my Voluntary Retirement.

Thus then I was relieved from my job on 31.12.2003.

Voluntary Retirement accepted and my dues payment were cleared in May 2004.

Then 1st thing I made, I cleared all my loan in one go and relieved of Debt worries.

1st elder daughter was already pursuing B. E. at Wardha.

2nd daughter Priyanka was selected for National Institute for Fashion Technology (NIFT), Banglore, was admitted in May 2004.

And thus all admission of kids were secured in 2004-2005 session.

On Central Railway many positions for Doctors were vacant. There were recruitment of C.M.P. (Contract Medical Practitioner) open in month of September 2004.

I had attended the interview and selected for C.M.P. post and posted me at Miraj, Pune Division of Central Railway.

Now I was availing my Pension with additional contract amount.

Thus I had taken the decision which nobody was even thinking. No one was on my side, I stand alone to fight crisis as I was clear in my mind, that what step I am going to take may put me in trouble, but prepared myself for the worst and carried out my decision, immediately once finalized in my mind. In this decision, I applied both techniques.

1.   Live in Water tight compartment.

2.   Anti worrying technique of Mr. Willis H. Carries.

Dr. A Lexis Carrier, Nobel Prize winner in Medicine said, "Those who don't know how to fight worry die young." Businessmen, Housewives, House Doctors and many more.

Dr. O. F. Cober chief physician of gulf said, "Seventy percent (70%) patients cure themselves if only they got out of their fears and worries. Nervous indigestion, Nervous diarrhoea some stomach ulcers, Heart diseases, insomnia, some headaches etc.

Fear causes worrying, worry makes tense, stressed, nervous and affect your nerves of stomach, which in turn changes gastric secretions from normal to abnormal which often leads to gastric ulcers.

Dr. Joseph F. Montague said, "You don't get stomach ulcers from what you eat, you get ulcers from what is eating you."

Dr. W. C. Alvarez of Mayo Clinic said, "Gastric ulcers frequently flares up or subsides according to hills and valleys of emotions and stress. It has known connection with mood, emotional status. This statement is backed by 15,000 patients treated at Mayo Clinic for stomach ulcers 4 out of 5 patients had no physical basis for their gastric illness.

Fear, worry, hate, supreme selfishness, and inability to adjust themselves to the reality of world, these were the causes of stomach illnesses and ultimately of gastric ulcers, such gastric ulcers can kill.

According to Life Magazine, they now stand with in our fatal list of diseases.

Dr. Harold C. Hibein of Mayo Clinic who read paper of Annual Meeting of Association of Industrialist, physician and surgeons. He said, "In his study of 176, Business executions average age of 43.3 years. He reported slightly more than 1/3 i.e. 35% suffered from one of three aliments peculiar to high tensions living.

1. Heart Disease

2. Digestive track Disease

3. Hypertension.

What shall it profit a man if he gains whole world and loose his health. Even if you own the whole world, he could sleep in one bed at a time, and only need 3 meals.

So I will prefer to be care free person, with no responsibility than wreak my health of 45 years of age; by trying to build big organization of cost of health and life. Any thing that cost your peace and health is too expensive.

In stead of trading years of life to what is called business success, tension free care free life is more precious.

From above statement, it proves that, if for earning more and more if you loose your health and life is not at all worthy. As far as your health permits, it has not causing any adverse effect, tension, worries, then you are in your limits of good achievement.

Do not compromise your health for sake of money or worldly things.

We can buy with money, good living home, a very comfortable bed, but not sleep. I do not mean do not make efforts to earn, but not at cost of health and peace of mind.

William James said, "God may forgive us our sins, but nervous system does not."

It shows if we allow our stress and strains beyond it's accommodative limits our nervous system will label and it will throw us in tension, anxiety, depression and what not. Hence be in your tolerable limits, so as to keep yourself calm, peaceful, tension free in order to maintain good health.

Here is a starling and most incredible facts, "More Americans commit suicide each year than die from five most common communicable disease" as we have seen from statistics. Why? The answer is largely worry.

Worry is like constant drip-drip-drip of water, constant drip-drip of worry drives men to insanity and suicide. Hence if you are chronic worrier, you may develop Angina, Hypertension, Insomnia, some day or other.

If you love life, want to live long and healthy "STOP Worrying".

Dr. Alexis Earrel said, "Those who keep the peace of mind of their inner self in midst of tumult of modern city are immune from nervous diseases."

"Train your mind to be clam in every situations."

So don't loose control over your mind be calm, peaceful, your inner self will be happy and you will live life with all your enjoyments.

Thoser Said, "Most of us are stronger than we realise" We have inner resources, that we have never tapped.

It is always said and proved fact that your brain have tremendous power like a power house, which can generate lot of energy when you use it. It is further said, No genius even utilized brain power more than 12-13%. Ordinary people generally use 2-3% of brain capacity in their life. It proves you have great powerhouse to be tapped.

Walden Said, "I know of no more encouraging fact than the unquestionable ability of human to elevate his life, he has imagined. He will meet sucess, unexpected in common hours."

As advised by Dr. Kellog, "Face Facts", Quit worrying, then do something cheerful. Cheerful attitude gives courage to fight with any adverse situation."

That means, unless you understand your own problem, there you cannot find it's solution. Unless or diagnose the cause of diseases, he will not be able to treat so you must stop worrying; as 1st step collect all the facts, put them in order of priority, understand root cause and it will enable to find remedy. Hence instead of worrying, calm your conscious, concentrate on removal of cause and then and there it gets solved.

As per famous Mayo brothers who declared that more than half of our hospital beds are occupied by nervous patients, yet when nerves of these patients studied, under high power microscope, after postmortems examination there nerves found healthy, in most of the cases; that nervous trouble caused was not due to physical, organic deterioration of nerves, but emotions of fatality as frustration; anxiety, fear, depression and despair.

Plato said, "That greatest mistake physicians make is that they attempt to cure body organs, without attempting to cure mind, supreme controller of body."

So, understand "Body and mind as one, and should not be treated separately."

As it is said, "Fear is greatest enemy of mankind." Fearful mind loose control of decision making power, it goes against your intelligence and capacity, which makes blunders, so do not afraid off any situation. Let sometime pass, let situation get diluted. If it is not under your control, let it be. Time will solve it.

Body and mind works in coordination and together. It took world medical science more than 200 years to recognize this great truth. As yet Indian Medical system has not considered this aspect even till date. Medical curriculum is not yet serious to think on psychological, philosophical aspect of medical science. No stress is given to develop curriculum in medical education while educating medical graduates.

Our Indian Doctors still treat only organs without applying mind to rational logical approach to see causes of Hypertension which are largely due to maladjustment to life situation, rather than physical origin and placed on medication, which in turn starts worries of their illness and life long medications, which again aggravates psychological pressure, add to agony rather than improvement. The brain gets aware of hypertension, life long treatment they become self centered.

So now stress to be given on psychological aspects on the subject and if treated logically, counselling and removal of root cause of worries, will help much to the patients.

As modern medical science largely wiped out diseases caused by physical causes like bacteria, viruses after advent of antibiotics and immunization. But still medical science has been unable to cope with mental healing and psychological wreaks caused by emotions worry, fear, hate, frustration and despair casualties caused by these mental emotional diseases are mounting and spreading with catastrophic rapidity, which needs timely attention. Hence we will have to upgrade our approach and improve medical care system.

As we are still physical level thinkers, doctors, policy makers will have to change their mental attitude, perception while treating human in totality, which needs changes at expert level while formulating medical curriculum.

Our medical universities, medical college heads, educationist will have to think deeply on subject and carefully introduce psychology and philosophy for rational logical development of medical student.

What causes Insanity?

Nobody knows exact reason, but in most of the cases contributing factors are insecurity feeling, fear, worry, anxiety, harassed individual who is unable to cope with reality of world and retreats into the private dreamy world of his own making, which he thinks may solve his worries.

Ref. Book - Dr. Edward Podolsky

"STOP WORRYING AND GET WELL"

Capters :- 1) What worry does to Heart?

2) High B.P. is fed by worry.

3) Rheumatism can be caused by worry

4) Worry less for your stomach sake

5) How worry can cause cold?

6) Worry and Thyroid

7) The worrying diabetics

Book by Dr. Karl Menningers

1) Man against himself

2) Mayo brothers psychiatry

It is starling revelation, How we destroy our bodies and minds by anxiety, frustration, hatred, resentment, rebellion etc.

In our Indian scriptures we find, six enemies of mankind.

काम, क्रोध, माया, मोह, मद, मत्सर

Worry can put you in wheel chair with rheumatism and arthritis.

Dr. Rusell L. Caril world recognized authority on Arthritis had listed 4 common conditions that bring on Arthritis.

1) Martial ship wreak

2) Financial Disasters and grief

3) Loneliness and worry

4) Long cherished Resentment

These are not only causes of Arthritis, but commonest conditions associated with Arthritis patients.

Dr. William I. L. Mc. Gonigle said, in his address to American Dental Association that "Unpleasant Emotions such as worry, fear, nagging may upset calcium balance can cause tooth decay."

Dr. Israel Bram a famous Thyroid specialist and treating such elements from years together wrote, "Emotional upset may trigger Thyroid Dysfunctions."

ಐ ಐ ● ಚ ಚ

8. RELAXATION AND RECREATION

The most relaxing and recreating forces for good health.

Sleep, Music, Laughter, Religion.

Have faith in GOD

Learn to sleep well

Love good music

See funny side of life

And Health and Happiness be yours.

Film star Merle Oberon, she told that, she refused to worry because she knew that worry will destroy. Le Chief asset on motion picture screen i.e. "HerLook". Nothing can destroy her look as quickly as worry. Worry curdles expressions. It may turn grey hair, even hair fall. It can ruin complexion, arise eruptions and pimples etc.

So quit worrying and be Healthy and Happy.

Rudyyard Kipling said, "I keep six Honest, serving men, they taught me all I knew.

They are "What", "When", "Why", "How", "Who", "Where"

क्या, क्यो, कब, कैसे, कहाँ और कौन

These are not only words but are teachers, when properly analyzed and carefully listened.

How to analyze problem?

Aristotle   1) Get the facts

          2) Analyze the facts

          3) Arrive at decision and Act on it.

1) Get the facts :-

Unless you have facts, it will not be possible even to attempt to solve the problem intelligently. Without facts our mind is in confusion.

It was the idea of Herbert E. Hawks, Dean of Columbia College of Columbia University. He said, "Confusion is the main cause of worry." 50% of worry is causal by people trying to make decision before they have sufficient knowledge on which to base a decision. He said, "I don't agonize over my problem. I don't loose my sleep, simply concentrate on getting the facts if I have got all the facts, the problem usually solves itself."

He further said, "That if a man will devote his time to secure facts in an impartial, objective way, his worry will evaporate in the light of knowledge."

We need only the facts that justify our acts. The facts that fit in conveniently with our wishful thinking and justify our pre-conceived prejudices.

Andre Marrois wrote, "Everything that is in agreement with our personal desires seems true."

We have to keep our emotions out of our thinking and as Dean Hawks said, "We must secure facts in an impartial objective manner."

2) Analyze the Facts :-

It is easier to analyze facts after writing down.

As Charles Kettering put it "A problem well stated is problem half solved." Ask 2 questions to yourself.

Q. 1 What I am worrying about?

Q. 2 What can I do about it?

Experience proved time and after enormous value of asking at a decision. 50% worries vanishes. If a clear definite decision is arrived, 40% worries disappear. When you start carry out your decision.

Galen Litchfield Technique to stop worrying

a)   Write down precisely What am I worrying about?

b)   What can I do about it?

c)   Decide what to do?

d)   Start immediately to carry out decision.

The method is superb, it is effective efficient, concrete and goes directly to the heart of problem.

William James said, "When once a decision is reached after analyzing facts and execution is in order of the day. Dismiss absolutely all responsibilities and care about outcome.

He emphasized when you made careful decision based on facts, go into action. Don't stop to reconsideration. Don't begin to hesitate, Don't loose yourself in self doubting. Don't keep looking back over your shoulder.

Now, we will see how do deal with our problem.

Pendown :-

What is the exact problem?

What are the possible solution?

What solution best suits me?

Make your own assessment and decision. Act quickly with confidence without delay. It will solve your problem in due course of time.

HOW TO BREAK WORRYING HABIT?

Before it breaks you

Keep yourself busy, engaged, so no time to worry.

How it Acts?

As per law, it is utterly impossible for any human mind, no matter how brilliant, to think more than one thing at a given time.

One kind of emotion drives out other psychoneurotic prescription keep them busy, that is called "occupational Therapy".

Psychiatrist feels "Keeping Busy" is one of the best anaesthetic ever known for sick nerves. When we are not busy; our mind tend to become a near vacuum which is filled by nature with emotions. Emotion of worry, fear, hate, jealousy, envy. These emotions are so violent that they tend to drive out of your minds; all peaceful happy thoughts and motions.

James L. Mursell Professor of Education Teachers College, Columbia said, "Worry is most apart to ride you, nagged, not when you are in action, but when the day work is done. Your imagination can run riot then bring up all sorts of ridiculous possibilities and magnify each little blunder. At such time, your mind is like motor operating without it's load. It races and threatens to burn out it's bearing, or even tear itself to bits."

Hence remedy for worry is to get completely occupied doing something constructive. Without purpose the days would have ended as such as always end in disintegration.

Dr. Richard C. Cabol, formerly professor of Clinical Medicine at Harward in his book, "What men live by" says, "As a physician, I have had the happiness of seeking work cure many persons, who have suffered from trembling palsy of the soul, which results from over mastering doubts, hesitation, vaccination and fear courage given us by our work is like self-reliance, which Emerson has made for ever glorious."

As Charles Darwin said, "Wibber, Gibbers : Wibber, Gibbers are out fashioned grumbling that will run us hollow and destroy our power of action, and our power of will.

George Bernard Shaw said, "One secret is being miserable is to have Leisure to bother about, whether you are happy or not."

So don't bother to think about, split on your hands and get busy. Your blood will start circulating your mind, your mind will start ticking, pretty soon. This whole positive upsurge of life in your body will drive worry out from your mind."

"Get Busy," "Keep Busy". It is cheapest kind of medicine, there is on this earth and one of the Best.

Rule : "Keep Busy" The worried person must loose himself in Action, Last he wither in dispair.

Judge Joseph of Chicago after acting arbitrator in more than 40,000 cases of unhappy marriage declared. "Trivialities are at the bottom of most unhappy marriages."

As our mind after marriages are preoccupied by expectation from our partner rather than giving.

Expectation which are not full filled causes distraction, unhappiness and start going against each others. Nobody can fulfill others expectations each and every desire at each and every time. It is never possible for anybody to satisfy your wishes, wills because desires have no limits if one is fulfilled, other always ready to enter in your mind.

In Indian Perspective most of the couples divided mentally because of doubts about spouses sexuality. As a male and female thinking pattern are always different in this respect.

Our culture is so rigid that once married means, no separation, how much mismatching may be there and then if once gap of understanding start it widen mostly rather than closing, because each ones ego start operating. As preoccupied minds then did not allow them coming closure to even dialog. They both starts thinking in their own ways and perception are always different, Leading to unhappy marriages.

District Atomey of New York county Frank S. Hogan said, "Fully half of the cases in our criminal courts originates in little things. It is small blows to our self esteem, that indignities little Jolts to our vanity which causes half of the heart pains in the world."

A well-known legal magazine says, "De minimus non curat Lex" that means, the law does not concern itself with trifles and neighter should be worried, if he wants peace of mind."

Law cannot save marriages it can only prevent divorces, i.e. physical separation, giving trial living togather, but if you really want to be together then the couple itself must accept their own mistakes, mismatching views, and try to give rather than demand. The thoughts of togetherness must be from both parties. Some where they have to be willing to compromise with their own perspectives. Much of the time, all we need to overcome the annoyance of trifles, is effect of shuffling of emphasis set up a new pleasurable point of view in the mind. It is with many worries, we dislike them and get them into at start, all because we exaggerates their importance.

Disral said, "Life is too short to be little."

So we are on the earth for few decades, just to live, out of that we have already crossed some. There must not be dissatisfaction and worry. You have to conqure your worries what ever it may be because life is too short to be little, and I have no time to battle egos and small minds.

Andee Maurosis said, "Often we allow ourselves to be upset by small things, we should despise and target. As we are on the earth only few decades to live and we loose many irreplicable hours brooding over grievances that in a year time will be forgotten by us and by everybody. Human mind is such it forget very easily, what they receive but thinks about deficiencies and keep mind filled with it. So let us devote our lives to worth while actions and feelings to great thoughts real affections and enduring undertaking. "For life is too short, to be little."

"So brake worry habits, before it brakes you." So the rule is "Let's not allow ourselves to be upset by small things, we should despise and forget, Remember "Life is too short, to be little."

Do not be a begger of love, be a donor of love, beautiful people are not always good; but good people are always beautiful.

Life is short, spend it with people who makes you laugh and feel loved.

ಐಐ ● ಚಚ

9. The Law of Averages

It is stated that, nearly all our worries and unhappiness come from imagination and not from reality.

Let's examine the record, Let's ask ourselves "What are the chances according to the law of averages, that this event, I am worrying about will ever occur.

Co operate with the inevitable . William James said, "Be willing to have it so." Acceptance is what has happened is the first step to overcome the consequences of any misfortune."

So we must learn sooner or later that we must cooperate and accept with inevitable. It is so if it cannot be otherwise.

This means, we cannot avoid the happening many a times. The events which are bound to happen and we don't have control over it, we should prepare our mind to accept and cooperate with it.

The Late Gorge V had these framed words hanging on wall of his Library in Bukimgham Palace, "Teach me neither to cry for moon nor over split milk."

Schopenhaur in his way said, "A good supply of resignation is of first importance in providing for journey of life."

Obviously circumstances done don't make us unhappy, it is the way we react to circumstances that determines out feeling. It is just our reaction to any situation which decide, the outcome whether you mentally strong enough to sustain the blow or not. If you strongly with yours ability sustain the trauma, you will not be in very bad situation. If you resist, then outcome will be in your favour. Unhappiness trickles only, when you allow it to hurt you. Prepare your mind to fight any situation and it will disappear.

Jesus said, "The kingdom of Heaven is with you, where the kingdom of hell is too."

We can all endure disaster and tragedy and triumph over them. We may not think we can, but surprisingly strong inner resources that will see us through, if we make use of it, We are stronger than we think. Trust yourself, you have survived a lot and will survive, what ever is coming.

Tarkington said, "If I lost all of my five senses, I know I would live on inside my mind; for it is in mind, we see; and in mind we live. Whether we know it or not."

That the acceptance of circumstances. It taught him as Jonson Milton discovered. It is not measurable to be mind, but it is only measurable not to be able to think of blindness.

Late Dean Hawker of Columbia University told, that had taken a mother goose Rhyme as one of his mottoes.

For every ailment under the Sun
There is a remedy, or there in none
If there is one, try to find it
If there is none, never mind it

From above it is clear that if there is a solution to your problem, worries you find it with utmost sincerely. If you cannot, then leave it to the time, and accept as it is.

Henry Ford said, "If I can't handle the events, I let them handle it self."

It means if I have no control over the happening then Let it go in it's way, instead of worrying about it.

K. T. Keller, then president of Chryster Co-operation said, "When I am up against a tough situation; if I can do anything about it, I do it. If I cannot do, I just forget it. I never worry about the future because I know, no man living can figure out what is going to happen in future. There are so many forces that will affect the future! Nobody can tell that what prompts those forces or understand them.

Hence worry about future is myth.

Epictetus taughts to Romans, there is only one way to happiness, that is to cease worrying, the things, beyond power of our will.

So worrying is no remedy, nor beneficial in any sense.

STOP worrying will lead to peace if not remedy.

Elsie Mac Cormic said, "When we stop fighting the inevitable, we release energy, which enable us to create a richer life. No one living has enough emotions and vigor to fight the inevitable and at the same time, enough left over to create a new life. It is a choice, you can bend with inevitable sleet storms of life or can resist them and break.

So it will be wise to accept inevitable, to prevent breakage of ourselves.

The Masters of Jutitsu teach their student, "To bend like the willow; Do not resist like a Oak."

So be flexible enough to receive blows than to resist if cannot be sustainable. If you learn to absorb shocks and Jolts along the rocky roads of life. You will last longer and enjoy smoother ride.

If you resist inevitable it will bring series of inner conflicts causing you worries, tension, strain and be neurotic. If you go still further and reject harsh world of reality, retreat into a dream of your thinking, making you insane.

The following Priceless poem written by Dr. Reincold Nebuhr, "God grant me the serenity to accept the things, I cannot change, courage to change the things, I can, and wisdom to know the difference."

It is clear from that every grate philosopher agreed that, there are certain situation, which are not under control to be changed, are to be accepted at it is, otherwise that will break you and your life.

Human Hesse, "Love your suffering. Do not resist it, do not flee from it. It is only your aversion to it that hunts, nothing else."

ಬಲಬಲ●ಜಲಜ

10. STOPLOSS

I put a stoploss order on every market commitment, I make said, Bulrton S. Castles a reputed stock player. If your commitments are intelligently made in first place your profit will average 10, 25, 50% or more, consequently by limiting your losses to 5% you can be wrong more than half of the time and still make plenty of money. This same principle can be applied to your worries also.

As Lincon said, "A man does not have time to spend, half his life in quarrels, if anybody ceases to attack me. I never remember at the past against him.

Whenever we are tempted to throw good money after bad, in terms of human living. Let's stop and ask ourselves, How much this thing, I am worrying about really matter?

At what point shall I set a stoploss on this worry, and forget it. Exactly how much should I pay for this. Have I already paid more than it's worth.

Don't try to sow, saw dust Don't cry for split milk. This means, whenever you are in situation, which is disturbing you and you had worried much for. Still you are bothering for it. It is not wise to continue about the same.

You might had paid much penalty in any form or other. You might got much disturbed, but you have to stop some where and this is moment you should.

Once milk split, don't cry for it, forget it and concentrate on some other doings.

As Shakespear advised wise men never sit and wait their losses but early seek how to redress their harm.

Let the past bury, it is dead. Don't sow saw dust.

A great philosopher who rules Roman Empire Marcus Aurcelus said, "Our life is, what our thought makes it."

If we think happy, cheerful thoughts, we will be happy and cheerful. If we think miserable thoughts, we will be miserable. It depends on your mental perception. If we think only about deficiency we will find lot of it, but if we look for what we have and think it ample, we will not need much, you will be satisfied and will be able to enjoy your belongings.

If we think of some sort of fear the thoughts of fear, will make we fearful. If we think of sickness, we will feel as sick. If we dream losses, we will loose.

Hence it is very much necessary to be positive in mind. Negativism of thoughts cannot bring up yourself. Positive thinking will let you do everything better than negative thinking will.

Norman Vincent Peale said, "You are not what you think you are; but what you think, you are."

If you stay positive in negative situation, you win.

Your thoughts decides your personality your attitude towards your life, whether positive or negative make your personality like wise.

Hence we must assume positive attitude. In other words, we need to be concerned about problem, but not worried. Our mental attitude has almost unbelievable effect on our physical power.

The famous British Psychiatrist J. A. Hodfield gives striking illustration of just in his booklet, "The psychology of power." He wrote, "I asked 3 men to submit themselves to test the effect of mental suggestion by gripping Dynomanometer with all their might. He had then repeated under three different set of conditions.

a)	Under normal condition grip was 101 Lb.

b)	After Hypnotism with suggestion of weakness grip was 29 Lb.

c)	Under Hypnotism suggestion of strong, powerful, grip was 142 Lb.

When their mind were filled with positive suggestion of strength, that increase their physical power almost 40%.

But when suggestion were negative and weakness to power almost reducing by 70%. It proves that negativism damages more, Physical power is lost much.

"Such is incredible power of Mental attitude."

This experiment shows, that if you think, you are weak, you loose much of your power and feel very weak.

On the contrary if you think you are strong and powerful, then your physical power increases and you feel powerful.

As per Saint Mathew, Bible words, "And behold they brought to him, a person sick of palsy; lying on bed and Jesus said, unto the sick of palsy. Son be of good cheer, thy sin be forgiven, thee arise take up thy bad and go unto thine house and be arouse. These words of Jesus produced such strrength in the Mrs. Eddy [Marry Baker Eddy] who was sick with spinal Palsy due to injury, was poor having no shelter and food due to poverty, that she immediately got out of bed and walked.

Your mental power can make such miracles, if you give suggestions to your mind.

That experience Mrs. Eddy declared was falling Apple that let me to discovery of how to be well myself, and how to make others too. I gained the scientific certainty that all causation was mind and every effect as "Mental Phenomena".

As such was the way Mrs. Mary Baker Eddy became founder of high pristress of new religion, that had encircled the globe.

Such tremendous power is in thoughts, It is a power house which everybody possess.

Hence, change the thoughts, mental attitude, mental thinking pattern. In such way each and everybody can transform his / her life. Such transformation can lead to more productive and happy life, not only for yourself but for those around you, it an enlightenment.

"As a man thinketh in his heart so, he is."

The peace of mind, joy we get out of living depends not on, where we are what we have or who we are but solely upon our mental attitude. Outward conditions have very little bearing on us.

Every thing in your life is a reflection of a choice you have made. If you want different result, make a different choice. Your mind can change your life.

Do every thing with a good heart and expect nothing in return and you will never be disappointed.

If we cherish creative thoughts of courage and calmness, we can really enjoy scenery while sitting on our coffin riding to gallows or we can fill our tents with singing songs of cheer while starring and freezing to death.

Mr. Milton in his blindness discovered some truth 300 years ago.

"The mind is it's own place and in itself.

Can make a heaven of Hell or Hell of Heaven."

From above discussion, it is clear that nothing can bring you peace, but yourself.

Emerson noted this in his assay on self reliance.

Epictetus stoic philosopher warned, "That we ought to be

more concerned about removing wrong thoughts from mind, than about removing tumors and abscesses from the body."

In modern medicine Dr. G. Canby Robinson declared that 4 out of 5 patients admitted to John Hopkins Hospital were suffering from condition brought impart by emotional strains and stresses. This is often true even in cases of organic, disturbances, eventually. He declared, "These trans back to maladjustment to life and it's problems."

Montaigne the grate French philosopher adopted his life motto as "A man is not hurt so much by happing but as by his opinion of what happens is entirely up to us."

Any event, any situation happened, which bothers you, when you take it as worry. That happening may not be serious or disturbing so much but our reaction and mental acceptance must be lacking.

If you think, you can manage the situation, only then your pattern of thinking to accept and solve the problem, thus mental attitude will bring you out of such situations, which will not hurt you so much. Now question arises.

Can we change our mental attitude by an effort of the will?

Answer is precisely, "Yes".

William James Practical psychologist once made this observation, "Action seems to follow feeling, but really action and feeling go together hand in hand, regulating the action which is under our control of the will. We can directly regulate the feelings which is not under direct control by controlling actions.

Thus he explains the sovereign voluntary path to cheerfulness, if your cheerfulness be lost, sit cheerfully to act and speak as if cheerfulness is already there.

It is physically impossible of remain blue or depressed, while you are acting out the symptoms of being radiantly happy. This is one of the basic truth of nature that can easily work miracles in all our lives.

As William James said, "Much of what we call evil, can often be converted into bracing and tonic good by a simple change of sufferer's inner attitude from one fear to one of fights."

So let's fight unhappiness by programming ourselves of cheerful and constructive thinking.

Rule -

"Think and Act cheerfully, and you will feel cheerful."

On the contrary, when we hate our enemy, we are giving them power over us, power over our sleep, our apetite, our blood pressure, our health and happiness.

Because by keeping hate and envy in our mind, we constantly think of them, which disturb our mind only, without affecting them and loose ourselves by all means.

Our enemies would dance with joy if only they knew, how they were worrying you, lacerating you, and getting even with us. Our hate is not hurting them at all, but our hate is turning our own days and nights into hellish turmoil, who do you suppose set this, ourselves who harbour hate and envy in our mind.

If selfish people try to take advantage of you, cross them of yours list, but don't try to get even. When we try to set even, we hurt ourselves, because they gain their way into ours mind, which is very harmful for our health, will in turn cause worry.

The main personality characteristics of person with high blood pressure is resentment. When resentment is chronic, hypertension follows, in next stage it will affect your heart.

Hence Jesus said, "Love your enemies." Forgive enemies as much as you can. This will keep you away from high stress syndrome."

Many people have wrinkled and hardened by hate, and disfigured by resentment. Hate destroys ability to enjoy even our food and our sleep.

This means simple food served with love is far better than lot of sweet dishes served with hatred in mind. Even if you can't love your enemy, at least you can love yourself.

Don't permit your enemy to control your happiness, health and sleep and your look. So if we can't love enemy, forget and forgive them for our own sake, and for our own interest.

Confucius said, "To be wronged, or robbed is nothing unless you continue to remember them."

A man is fool who don't angry, but A man is wise who won't be angry.

Train your mind to be calm in any situation. Avoid anger, when provoked. Stay positive in any negative situation you win.

A German Philosopher and author of studies in pessimism. He regarded life as futile and painful adventure, he said, "If possible no animosity should be felt for anyone."

Benard Baruh advisor of 6 presidents Wilson, Hording, Collidge, Hoover, Roosevelt and Truman said, "No man can humiliate or disturb you, unless we let him. Sticks and stones may break my bones, but words can never hurt me."

It means if you don't allow ourselves to hurt by others words, what ever they say, critisize or bluntly abuse, if you don't allow your mind to react them, then their words will be invain and you will be safe, undisturbed.

You are strongest, when you are calm. Epictetus pointed out nineteen century ago that, "We reap, what we sow; and some how fate almost always makes us pay mutefaction he further said, "Every man, penalty for his own deeds."

Bhagawat Geeta also endorses, "Our deeds decides our fate." कर्म सिध्दांत, (जैसा कर्म वैसा फल)

"How you sow, you will reap?"

The man who remember this will not be angry with anyone. Indignant with no one, Revile no one, Blame no one, offend no one and hate no one.

To cultivate mental attitude that brings peace and happiness.

Rule :

a)   *Let's never try to get even with our enemy.*

b)   *Let's never waste a minute thinking about people, we don't like.*

In Jesus words, "Love your enemy, bless them that curse you. Do good to them, that hate you and pray for them who despitefully use you and persecute you."

৪০৪০●৪৩৪৩

11. WORRY About Ingratitude

"Gratitude is a fruit of grate cultivation, you don't find it among gross people."

"Let's not expect gratitude from general cheist, laped to lopers in a day but only thanked him. i.e. 10%; so do how can we expect more than cheist."

Angry man; confucius said is always full of poison. It is natural for people to forget to be grateful, so if we go around expecting gratitude, we are headed straight for lot of headaches.

If you want to find happiness, Let's stop thinking about gratitude or ingratitude and give for inner joy of giving.

Gratitude is like a rose, It has to be fed, watered and cultivated, then loved and protected.

If our children are ungrateful, who has to be blamed? May be we are. If we have never taught them to express gratitude to others, then how can we expect to be grateful to us.

It is very rare phenomena to be grateful, as general human tendency is opportunistic. They will show interest, when in need and are sure, you will be one to full fill their need and element, But after receiving favour from you, they will easily forget it; without showing gratitude.

If we want our children to be grateful we must train them to be grateful, but generally it is taken for granted that it's duty of parents to fulfill all the needs, wants and desires. After getting older; they do not realize that they should show gratitude towards parents, unless you have taught them in childhood. So you have to cultivate this habit to be grateful since their primary days.

"I had the blues, because I had no shoes, until upon the

street, I met a man who had no feet."

As Eddie Richenbacken said, "The biggest lesson I learnt from experience was that if you have all the fresh water to drink, all good food to eat; you ought never to complain about anything."

About 90% of things in our lives are right and 10% are wrong or deficient. If you want to be happy, concentrate 90% which are right and in your possession for it's use, and ignore 10% that's wrong or deficient. If you want to be worried and bitter all you have to concentrate on 10% and ignore 90%, that is glorious. "Think and Think" Think of all you have to be grateful for and thank GOD for all our boons and botties."

Jonathan Swift author of "Gulliver's Travel" was most devastating pessimist also praised the great health giving powers of cheerful and happiness.

"The Best Doctor in the world, he declared are Doctor Diet, Doctor Quiet and Doctor Merrymen."

Be happy with what you have, you have all the riches in form of active body and mind, but do we appreciate all this?

I remember a Movie in Hindi titled "DHANWAN" Rajesh Khanna, the then superstar of hindi cinema, he acted as super rich, businessman. His life style was so amazing, that every luxury at his feet available, he had at least 50 male and female servants for his services, Every desire was full filled at just he orders. He them in his mind became so egoist that he can buy any thing, he desires, within no time.

Unfortunately then he met with an accident, and lost his vision of his injuries. As he was assuming that he could by anything with his money, he ordered his staff to by some one to donate eyes at any cost. Any dam cost will be given, who would donate his eyes, a big compensation declared through media, newspaper whatever way he could publish his requirement. But nobody turns in lastly he declared whole of his property for compensation, but nobody was willing for the deal.

Then he realized that worldly riches is not of that value, which he received from GOD. Then he realized that cost the body which he has, Then he realised that all his riches he cannot by A Eye, then he became grateful to GOD, who has given amazing wealth in form of active body and mind.

The moral of the story is nobody can buy single organ of his riches, so be grateful for what you have, you have all the riches inform of your active body and mind.

As Schopenhaur said, "We seldom think of what we have but always what we are lacking which is the greatest tragedy on our earth. This has caused many miseries, than all the wars and disease in history."

We can express only what is in our consciousness. Hence resolve to think only what you want thoughts of joy, happiness, health, lovely music, good songs, good food which you like, friends with whom you can enjoy, share feeling, inspiring books and planing a future with concentrated positive attitude for creative, purposeful, progressive and helpful life style.

Do good to some one, help to who you can, don't become self centered. Give smile, create smile on some ones face. If you will find pleasure helping others. Smile of other will give you satisfaction and happiness.

Dr. Samuel Johnson 200 years back said, "The habit of looking on the best side of every event is worth more than a thousand pounds a year."

So look that part of happening which are bright and ignore the dark part of it, as your vision and mission of life.

Logan Pearsull Smith said, "There are two things to aim

at in life, to get what you want, and after that enjoy it, only wisest man achieve the second."

Most of us just run behind accumulating year and year, but do not use it and let no body use it, just sit on it, and feel happy with possession of those accumulated wealth and lastly when you die, leave it all the others. That is only, pleasure of possession, no one can enjoy it till your life ends.

So you and I ought to be ashamed of ourselves, All the days of our years, we have been living in a fairy land of beauty. But have been too blind to see and too satiated to enjoy.

Rule :-

If you want to stop worrying and start living count your blessing, not your troubles.

12. Do Good To Others

It will come back in unexpected way As you know Life is an echo, We get what you give

In my medical job, I always tried to work sincerely and honestly. I use to treat my patients with best of my knowledge and efficiency.

But apart from that I remember two instances, when I was working at BAD station, near Mathura Junction. It was 8 km. away from Mathura Junction. There was no other medical facility available around other than Railway H. Unit. I was posted as A. D. M. O. Central Railway. In Railway colony around 400 Railway Quater were there with Railway staff and their families residing having population of 1500-2000.

And a very small Railway H. Unit with very limited facilities were there.

At one night say around 21 'O' clock, a child 10 months was bought to me crying since 2 hours consistently when I examined the child, no sign were available, expect irritated child.

So, I treated with some medicines, with advice that if baby does not get relief, please inform me after 2 hours for review.

But after that, they went at home. I was worried, I could not take rest and sleep, because I was worried about baby, but no message received up to morning 4 'O' clock. Then I personally went to the pharmacist and sent my pharmacist to stress the child at his residence; and collect information above baby's condition. They then said, "Baby got relief and become quite, sleeping calmly after 1/2 hour of my medication, they forget to inform me, then only I got relived.

Then I could go to my Quarter and took rest for 3 hours before to start my routine O.P.D.

In 2nd Incidence, which I faced, when I was working at Khandwa Junction. I received a call from station Manager, Message was passed from Itarsi.

Informing that A aged passenger in AC coach suffering from urinary problem not able to pass urine, need medical aid. When I attended on station, in train a well educated, qualified passenger traveling from Delhi to Banglore, identified as scientist in NCERT, was in agony as case of Retension of urine, with bladder full. After my examination, I said, "I would not be able to treat you on train. It will need surgical procedure i.e. catheterization.

I advised him to detrain immediately, I kept his baggage with station master and I personally on my two wheeler took him to Civil Hospital, Khandwa, in emergency called surgeon and then catheterization done and he was relieved his pain and agony. He was admitted for observation in Hospital, then went back to my home.

The help in such situation gives me satisfaction, and smile to my patients.

I also remember two-three instances when I got chance to help my colleague doctors.

When I was working at Central Railway Sub divisional Hospital Manmad Junction; as in charge hospital 1991-92.

Dr. Pichand recently joined as ADMO, Nandgaon which was under Central Railway division, Bhusawal, recently married. He was in need of 1 day leave to attend marriage of his brother in law. His leaves was regretted by M. S. Bhusawal, he was worried and he came to me at Manmad for help. We were 3 doctors at Manmad, against 4 posts and one vacancy.

Mr. Narsapur and Mrs. Narsapur, I called Dr. Narsapur, how can we help Dr. Pichand in this situation, I suggested Dr. Narsapur to manage, Nandgaon H. Unit against Dr. Pichand for a day. He showed inability to go to Nandgaon, as he had to prepare his son for school examination.

But I wanted to help Dr. Pichand, seeing his stress. I then agreed, I allowed Dr. Pichand to take leave and I went to Nandgaon to work against him.

2nd incidence, then I encountered with, when Dr. Narsapur and Mrs. Narsapur were in need of leave, to attend Marriage Ceremony at Aurangabad of Dr. Narsapur's Nephew.

I was sanctioning authority for casual leave up to 3 days. Dr. Mrs. Narsapur applied causal leave, which I had sanctioned. But Dr. Narsapur applied for A. P. L. (Average Pay Leave) for which sanctioning authority was M. S. Bhusawal, I had forwarded his application with note that relieving Doctor required if sanctioned. But as usual, M. S. / Bhusawal regretted Leave; as they were unable to arrange reliver from Bhusawal.

Dr. Narsapur became upset as the marriage was of his Nephew and he had to attend such close relatives ceremony. He discussed the matter with me, how can we manage this situation I wanted to relieve him from his anxiety. I suggested him to apply casual leave, which I can grant him leave. But problem was against 4 posts, can I manage Hospital and in case of untoward incident, how I will face the administration.

Finally I had decided to grant him one day causal leave, on my own risk and then he applied for C. L., which I granted and allowed him to attend ceremony.

One more incident, When Dr. Narsapur's father was critically ill, and he had to go to Gulburga (Karnataka) his hometown.

Unfortunately I was sick on that day and was on medical leave, Dr. Phadnis was Sr. D. M. O. in charge at sub divisional hospital Manmad, and I was under transfer order to WARDHA (Nagpur Division) but was yet to be relived.

As usual Dr. Mr. Narsapur applied for leave and also Mrs. Narsapur, both had to go. M. S. Bhusawal sanctioned leave for Dr. Narsapur on funny ground that Dr. Narsapur's father if critical, why Mrs. Narsapur has to go, let Dr. Narsapur go. They both were anxious, what to do now, M. S. Bhusawal not helping and rather causing Anxiety in such situation.

Then they came to me, as I was ill, and on medical leave. So, I advised them if required I am going to join even if I am sick, I would like to do duty, and help you.

But still M. S. Bhusawal was not ready to sanction her leave as they already regretted the leave, it was hurting their ego.

Then I had suggested Mrs. Narsapur to talk to C.M.D. Central Railway, Mumbai. Dr. V. D. Mathur was C.M.D. at that time and say, Dr. Hedaoo, even if sick agreed to join and willing to work against Dr. Mr. Narsapur. The C.M.D. allowed to Mrs. Narsapur to proceed on leave.

But unfortunately Dr. Narsapur's father expired before they reached there home.

Thus my motto of life, I maintained to help whenever I got chance to. It gives most satisfaction to our soul.

"The greatest gift you can give some one is your time, your attention, your love, your concern."

Once, I received a call from ASM/Manmand that, A person fall from train few kms. from station, and is injured and need medical aid. I attended on station, when I examined I found patient unconscious with Head injury. Immediately, I brought him to Railway Hospital and started treatment, but due to limited facilities at our hospital and seeing critical condition of the patient, I decided to shift him to Civil Hospital, Nasik for further treatment. He is being non Railway unknown passenger, he was not Railway beneficiary.

At about 8-9 p.m. I informed Station Manager and RPF that, patient is critical and hence to be shifted to Civil Hospital, Nasik by coming train.

I with my attendant, staff Nurse, accompanied patient in train and reached Nasik Road Station at around 10-10 p.m. Patient waa detrained at Nasik Road Station, when I requested to ASM, Nasik Road to arrange transfer of patient, to my surprise, no vehicle was available to shift in emergency due to political meeting of Mr. L. K. Adwani on that day, I was very much worried and helpless, his I. V. fluid was to finish with in 40-45 minutes.

I then went personally out side the station, but no vehicle was ready to move. No driver was willing to go because of security personal were not allowing them to move in the meantime. I searched a police officer and made him aware of situation. That gentleman called immediately his subordinate and arranged a vehicle to shift the critically ill patient around midnight, I with my staff accompanied that patient, got him admitted to Civil Hospital, Nasik Road. I paid transport charges from my own pocket and then relived of my anxiety and returned back by next train early in morning at Manmad. Thus I could by many hurdles help the unknown passenger.

A incident, I would like to narrate how I tried to help a passenger.

A call from station ASM, received by evening time. A passenger traveling from Bhusawal to Mumbai in first class, at that time Railway bogies were with first class non A.C. bogies suddenly fall ill, it was very hot summer when, I examined the patient in train found him unconscious and with Hyperpyrexia, diagnosed as Heat Stroke / Sun stroke. Immediately patient was detrained and shifted to Railway Hospital, Manmad. My senior was not happy with my decision because the patient was not Railway Beneficiary, so who will bear the cost of treatment and there was life at risk.

Any how, I started the treatment called physician from Manmad Town for consultation, and treatment continued. But problem was nobody was with him, and no address was available to contact. Then RPF was called my me, I requested them to investigate and make efforts to contact his relation. Then after searching his bagage we found some cards, on wireless Mumbai RPF tried their best and after midnight they could however contact relatives. I got call from his relative, that they will reach in the morning and requested me to treat patient with best possible, I assured them I am trying my level best to manage the situation. I could any how reduced the temperature, and his breathing rate heart rate was maintained normally; but his consciousness was not yet regained.

In morning his relative came and then I advised them to shift patient to higher center as at Manmad, no other hospital is well equiped to treat such condition and then they shifted the patient; which then relieved me, from my worries and anxiety after my whole night efforts, that gives great satisfaction of work.

"Where there is will there is way"

When I was working at Central Railway H. Unit, Satara during my posting as C.M.P.

I remember the incident, I was just seeing our H. Unit garden and planning plantation in premises of H. Unit.

Mr. Jagtap ASI RPF came to H. Unit, he was on duty and in uniform we were just talking about garden development. Just standing in shade. Suddenly Mr. Jagtap felt uneasiness and giddiness; when I saw to him, I immediately with the help of attendant made him, Lie down on bed.

On my examination, I suspected, he might have IHD (Ischemic Heart Disease), I immediately started, treatment and informed his S. I. about his illness I asked him to send two RPF constables as he will have to be shifted to Pune Railway Hospital for further investigation and consultation of cardiologist, I put him on sicklist, made arrangement to shift the patient by arriving train, under information to C.M.S. Pune requesting ambulance on station at Pune.

He reached Pune afternoon and then he immediately reffered to Budhrani Hospital, where cardiologist examined him, Angiography done, followed by Angioplasty and thus, he recovered and discharged after few days of treatment.

Thus helping timely has saved him but more than that, I found the pleasure of helping in time.

So, whenever, in any way, any kind of help given gives lot of satisfaction to our self. Where there is a will, there is Way." Always be ready to help anybody any where, which gives grate satisfaction & value of our own life.

My profession blessed me many chances to help, and I never loose any chance to grab it.

So everyone can be blessed with such chances to help some today of any kind of help, so grab it, it will give value to your life and great pleasure also.

13. Be Yourself Every One is Unique

The problem of being willing to be yourself is as old as history, says Dr. James Garden Gilkey and as universal as human life.

Angelo Patri wrote on subject of child training said, "Nobody is so miserable as he who tongs to be somebody else, and somebody other than person he is "body and mind."

Well known Hollywood Director Sam Wood said, "Greatest Headache, he has with aspiring young actors is exactly this, to make them be themselves."

Paul Boynton, then director employment of Major Oil Company who interviewed more than 60,000 job seekers and written a book entitled, "6 ways to get a job". He said, "Biggest mistake people make applying for job is not being themselves. They often try to give you answer, they think interviewer want; but it does not work, because nobody wants a phony; Nobody ever wants a counterfeit coin."

It means interviewer wants your own out look for which you have applied. How you will shoulder responsibility if rest on you. What efforts will you put to develop the organization. In other words how you fit for the job, and how you like to prove it. If your answer and strategy can satisfy the interviewer you will definitely seek the job.

The renowned William James was speaking at people; who had never found themselves, when he declared that average person develops only 10% of his or her latent mental abilities compared to what we ought to be.

He wrote "We are only half awake." We are making use of only small part of our physical and mental resources.

It is scientifically noted, the genius of the world also

applied 10-12% of mental ability. Such is powerhouse every human being possess, General population only found using 2-3% of their mental capacity during life time. Broadly speaking human individual thus live within their limits, Even they possess power of various sorts, which they habitually fail to use.

Science of Genetic also proves that you are, what you are as a result of 23 pairs of chromosomes contributed by your parents. 46 chromosomes with genetic codes determine what you inherit.

That means every individual is unique in character and behaviors. Unique in thoughts as well with abilities, you need to explore.

Every brain has tremendous power rather powerhouse, which is such a build up that huge store for knowledge, vast capacity to develop skill. Only thing is you should be prepared for exploration and utilization of it.

As Arman Schienfeld said, "Anywhere from score to hundred genes, 1 with a single gene in some cases able to change the whole life of an individual.

"We are fearfully and wonderfully made." The writer of "You and Heredity" Arman Schienfeld even further wrote "Mother and father met and mated, there is only one chance in 300000 billion, the person you would be born."

So it is impossible to create another you, in this world so everybody is unique.

Be yourself don't try to imitate other, as imitation does not succeed and never long lasting.

You are something new and unique, in this world and be glad of it. As you are unique, your capability is unique, so make most what nature gave you.

You must be what your experience, your environment and your heredity have made you. For better or worse you must cultivate your garden, you must play your own instrument in the orchestras of life.

You have to develop your own ways to lead your life, with what you have received, from the nature, inheritance and by your approach towards life, best out of it.

Emerson in his Essay "Self reliance" wrote "There is a time in every mans education, when to arrive at conviction that envy is ignorance; imitation is suicide, that must take himself for better or worse, as his position that through the wide universe is full of good. No carnel of nourishing corn can come to him through his soil bestowed on that plot of ground which is given him to fill. The power which resides in him is new in nature and none but he knows; what that is which he can do nor does, he knows until he has tried."

It means, A individual only know what is in his heart and mind, he is only the judge of his own capacities and abilities. He is one who can explore the best out of him and he must try for it.

To cultivate a mental attitude that will bring us peace of mind and freedom from worries.

Rule :

Let's not imitate others,
Let's find ourselves and be ourselves.

౭౦౭౦●౮౩౮౩

14. Religion and Spirituality For Defeating Worry

Santayana's word, "Man is not made to understand Life, but to Live Life." I have gone toward a new concept of religion. I am fretted in what religion does for me. That help me to riches, fuller happy life. But religion does far more than that bring spiritual values."

As William James put it, "A new zest for life, more life, a larger riches, more satisfying life. It gives me faith, hope, courage. It banishes tension. Anxieties, fears and worries. It gives purpose to life, a direction and motivation. It helps to create for self an oasis of peace, amidst the whirling sand of life. It vastly improves happiness and abounding health.

Erancis Bacon rightly said over 300 years before, "A little philosophy in clineth man's mind to atheism, but depth in philosophy, bring the mens mind about to religion."

The newest of all sciences psychiatry is teaching what Jesus taught, because psychiatrist realize that prayer and strong religious faith will banish the worries, anxieties, strains fear, that causes more than half of our illness.

They know as one of their leaders, Dr. A. A. Brill said, "Any one who is truly religious does not develop a neurosis, as he has faith in GOD, it's will. He trust decision thy and believes thy gave circumstances will also give solutions.

Henry ford, one of the greatest businessman in the world said, "I believe GOD is managing affairs and that he does not need any advise from me. With GOD in charge, I believe that everything will workout for the best in the end; so what is there to worry about."

Thus if you really have faith in GOD, who is Generator,

operator and destroyer, has made you to work for his plans, your life for your ultimate upliftment create situations, gives solution and forward you to achieve ultimate goal. Hence nobody has to worry as GOD is taking care off.

Many psychiatrists believe in prayer and faith. They are not advising to lead religious life; over to avoid hell fires in next world, but they are urging us to lead religious, spiritual life to avoid hell fires of stomach ulcers, angina, neurosis, breakdown and insanity, suicide stress, strains, fears and envy etc. which are mankinds true enemies.

Now psychologists and psychiatrist are teaching, "Return to Religion" Book by Hentry C. Link.

As Jesus taught, "Religion should exist for human, not human for subbath." He talked about fears of different kinds, that about sins "The wrong kind of fear is a sin. A sin against your health, a sin against riches, fuller happier courageous life, that Jesus advocated.

Emerson spoke of himself as a professor of science of joy. Jesus too was a teacher of science of joy. He commented his disciples to rejoice and leap for joy Jesus declared there were only two important things about religion.

a) Loving GOD with all your heart

b) Loving our neighbour and ourselves.

William James father of modern psychology wrote to his friends, professor Thomas Davidson saying, as years went by he found himself less blessed to get along with GOD.

Now question arises what is Religion? True religion, what it teaches us?

What is concept of religion?

Your perception to religion?

So it is very necessary to understand religion its effects

73

on human being.

How religions are created in the history of human race; purpose of religion?

The purpose of religion is to create a society with faith in creater, it should uplift, each and every human from its worries and show road to lead peaceful happy life, enrich and spread love for each other, those who believe in peaceful society.

How religions came into existance?

A person, deep thinker, experienced with life thoughfully put his principals, his concepts, and perception of life; and expected from followers to create peace and happiness for each fellow in and around.

But latter on for supreme selfishness few so called religious leaders, distorted the real object of the religion, and turn it to their gains, power, control over their disciples, followers during the course of time, distorted true purpose of religion and spirituality. They put forward the gains and losses after death in such fashion that influenced followers with dreamy world after death, as heven and hell.

They put in minds of their followers, that if you do such and such in the name of religion, you will be blessed with "Heaven" which will be full of happiness and that your destiny, Salvage (मोक्ष). You will be permanent in association of GOD and will be out of cycle of birth and death. These delusion are sowed in mind, who are not logical thinkers and blind followers.

Also they created 'Hell' and put fears in mind of the human who adopted their principles and advises; if they don't follow such and such, they will be put in Hell, where all sorts of punishments, painful for soul and will be sent back in cycle of birth and death starting from very-very low animal kingdom.

Such delusion fed in minds.

Thus delusion of supreme selfishness and or fears are formed in the minds who follows blindly these religious leaders.

These miths are very well depicted in films like 'OMG' "Oh My God" in which master actors like Paresh Rawal, Akshay Kumar, Mithun Chakraborty acted perfectly. Amir Khan also in "PK" tried to explore these wrong concepts of our religious leaders who misguides and distract the purpose meaning of religion.

So certain dangers are also associated with preaching of religion to common population, who blindly follow religious leaders and believes on stories they narrate causing delusion in mind. We have few examples of such religions so called God men. Asaram bapu and his son Narayan sai; Ram Rahim Sing, Baba Rampal and so on list may be long and when exposed, landed in prison.

Few muslim leaders so called mullas who through their misleading guidance created some extremism in the name of religion. So what I meant to explain that, it works as double edged sword and hence should be carefully, thoughtfully utilized for betterment of human race and not for destruction. So we must also consider there are few challenges hidden in such religion. Spiritual spirits which has to be believed and followed.

I don't want to go in controversies of different religions and faith. But my concept and perception is very dear about religion and spirituality that is "Humanity". I consider humanity as a only religion required for human race. In which every human should try to do good, help, spread love for others with selfless ness and with true heart.

दलाई लामा ''धर्म का अर्थ प्यार, करूणा,
मानवता, दयालुता और इन्सानियत फैलाना है।

So it is important while accepting religions advise also, don't blindly believe or follow think logically, human creation should be grateful to creator, should also prevent misconception and supreme selfishness. But have faith in GOD. The creator within the heart, soul there is no need to get associated to anybody if you truly have faith and belief in you and your protector.

My concept of Parmarth 'परमार्थ' is not to achieve our own dreamy gains and salvage but 'Parmarth' is one doing good, helping needy spreading love, uplifting somebody from his worries, understanding need of fellow human and trying to bring smile on some ones face. This will create a good humanity and it is the only religion and spirituality.

In simple words Parmarth is doing something for others, without self consideration with open heart, selflessly.

Supreme selflessness only can make every human being happy, cultivate such thoughts so that the world can be made fearless and for this prayers for every bodies good health, happiness will work wonders. The infinite source, supreme power will give mental, moral support provide fearless minds, encourgement to fight odd and strengthen your life with cheers. Prayers thus is a powerful tool to encourage human race to face any sort of situation and live life, enjoy living.

So it is necessary to understand and clear mind about religion and spirituality.

Rule :-

"Doing something good to bring smile on some ones face is true religion and spirituality."

संसार से भागे फिरते हो

संसार से भागे फिरते हो, भगवान को तुम क्या पाओगे

इस लोक को भी अपना ना सके, उस लोक मे पछताओगे ।।१।।

ये पाप हैं क्या ये पूण्य है क्या, रितो पर धर्म की मोहरे है

हर युग में बदलते धर्मो को, कैसे आदर्श बनाओगे ।।२।।

ये भोग भी एक तपस्या है, तुम त्याग के मारे क्या जानो

अपमान रचेता का होगा, रचना को अगर ठुकराओगे ।।३।।

हम कहते है ये जग अपना है, तुम कहते हो झूठा सपना है

हम जनम बिता कर जायेगे, तु जनम गँवा कर जाओगे ।।४।।

15. If you have Lemon Make Lemonade

The above advise was given by the late Julius Rosencold, President of Pears Kocback and Company to the chancellor Robert Maynard Hutchinson.

That is what a great Educator does to keep from worrying but the fool does exact opposite.

If he finds life has handed him Lemon, He gives up and says, "I am beaten, it is fate." I have got no chance. He proceed to behave against the world and indulge in an origy of self pity. But when a wise person handed a Lemon, he says, what lesson can't I learn from misfortune and How can I improve my situation? How can I turn this Lemon into Lemonade?

When I gone through the life of my father Late Pundlikrao M. Hedaoo, who wrote in his Biography "A Teacher", that when he was a toddler at the time of his father's demise, even he did not remember the face of his father. Mother was illiterate and working as daily wage labour. No one in family to guide. Nobody was literate in the family.

He narrated how he could get through such poverty with self struggle.

When he was studying in primary 3rd std. in the village.

His headmaster of primary school, asked him to appear for scholarship test, he agreed to appear and get through, that was in British era. He said this was the turning point of his life, for further education.

He took the chance and with the help of some donation, free ship from school authorities, some how he could finish his schooling and teachers training and got the chance to become a primary teacher at his hometown Shendurjana Ghat, Dist. Amravati. M. S. which was his birth place. Later in service he graduated and ultimately became Headmaster at the High School at Shendurjana Ghat.

But he never said, he had not got the chance, never regretted of situation. Thus he made Lemonade out of Lemon.

The grate psychologist Alfred Adher after studying people and their hidden reserve of power declared that one of the wonder filled characteristic of human being if their power to turn a minus to the plus.

Two men looked out from the prison bar, one saw the mud, and other saw the stars. That means how you see the world matters. What is your perception and perspective to visualize out of your thoughts? What you want to see whether is positive negative, bright or Dark, depends on your thoughts and pattern of your thinking.

There are two types of personalities, a Negative (Pessimist) and Positive (Optimist).

Now a days optimistic personalities are rare and pessimistic are all around. They never think of bright side of the things but always search for minus and exaggerates it. Always in doubts bad happing what ever may be the situation.

The Greeks taught 500 years before crist "The best things are most difficult." Harsy Emerson Fordick repeated its again in 20th century "Happiness is not mostly the pleasure, It is mostly victory." The victory that comes from senses of achievements and triumph of turning one "Lemon into Lemonade."

The late William Bolitho auther "Twelve against the GOD" put it like this "The most important thing in Life is not to capitalize on your gains; any fool can do it. The really important thing is profit from your losses, that requires intelligence and it makes the difference between men of sense and a fool."

That it is to use your ability and intelligence to turn your losses with spinning of your ideas to profits. A. L. Smith, not even finished graduate due to poverty had made his way with all his efforts to rise a best politician, Elected Governor of New York for 4 terms, a democratic candidate for president, six grate universities confirmed honourary degree including Columbia and Havard grate example of self made personality.

Shri. Narendra Modi, Prime Minister of India, also with grate difficulties from Tea Stall to Chief Minister of Gujrath and ultimately highest honor as Prime Minister of world's largest democracy for 2nd term.

Late Dr. Abdul Kalam Azad from a small village from Southern State of India with grate difficulties from childhood, to highest honor as President of India, Largest Democracy of the world.

Ramdeo Baba, founder of Patanjali Yog Peeth, along with Patanjali Industries having turn over of Rs. 1,00,00 Crs. per year, raised from rug of camping, and teaching Yoga turn in his fortune with his grate vision and ability.

Hollywood Actor Silvester Stallon, a Russian came at the age of 19 years to Hollywood with dream to become an actor. He tried his fortune in Hollywood for 10 years for his dream was rejected many-many times by established producers and directors. Then he himself produced a movie "Rocky" with all odds, which made his fortune in Hollywood and became a celebrity there after. He succeeded after long struggle of 10-12 years.

Founder of KFC, at the age of more than 60 years, retired from Military, who was living with difficulty after retirement, with just one Idea that he can prepare Fried Chicken very well.

He decided to work on his idea. He tried with many Hotel to introduce his recipe, but was rejected by many, even if he did not loose his heart, continued exploring some Dhabas and got an one. That recipe of his become so famous that he now has thousand of out lets all over the world.

There are so many examples those made Lemonade from Lemon.

Neitzscher's formula for superiority was not only to bear up under necessity, but to love it.

Most of the mens of achievement, carriers studies levels that surprisingly large number of them succeeded because they started with handicap that spared them on to grate endeavors, Grate Rewards.

If we go through life of Legendry Businessmen like Dhirubhai Ambani, Bill Gates, Warren Buffet, Henry Ford, Jac Ma Narayan Murthy, Asim Premji, TATAS, TESLA (Elon Musk) and so on.

All those created history in Business world with their vision, intelligence and ability to make Lemonade from Lemon.

As William James said, "Our every infirmities help us unexpectedly."

A great example of a scientist Stephen William Howkings who was diagnosed as motor neuron Paralysis when he was doing PHD, at the young age, then developed gradually whole muscular Paralysis. He was expected by experts that he will survive not more than 2-3 years. But fortunately he survived years together and with help of Technology he invented very useful fact in physics, Grate scientist in spite of his physical Infirmity.

Milton wrote better Poetry because he was blind.

Helen Kelter's brilliant Carrier was inspired, made possible in spite blindness and deafness.

Thchikovsy had been frustrated and driven to almost suicide by his tragic marriage, if his own life had not been pathetic, he possibly would never been able to compose his immortal "Symphonic Pathetique".

If Oostoevsky and Tolstoy had not been led tortured lives, they would probably never had been able to write immortal novels.

Saint Dnyaneshwar who wrote Dnyaneshwari had gone through many-many difficulties in his tender age, who was tortured by society, as being the son of a person who left married life in search of GOD, but reverted to married life afterwards, Even after so many difficulties Saint Dnyaneshwar wrote, Dnyaneshwari to throw light on Bhagvat Geeta's scripture and made it available to community who were not able to understand "Sanskrit" language. Dnyaneshwari for humanity and upliftment of community from dark to light.

Charles Darwin said, "If I had not been so grate as an invalid, I should not have been done so much work as I have accomplished."

Abraham Lincon, If he had been reared in an aristocratic family and had Law degree from Havard and happy married life. He would probably never had found in depth of his heart, the haunting words that he immortalized a Gelly shrug nor the sacred poem that he spoke at his second inauguration, the most beautiful and noble phrases, ever uttered by a ruler of man "With matice towards nor with charity for all."

Hary Emerson Fosdik in his book "The Power to see it through" says, "The north wind made the Viking, when ever did we get the idea that secure and pleasant living, the absence of difficulty, comfort of ease, ever if themselves people either good and happy upon contrary people who pity themselves go on pitying themselves even when they are led softly on a cushion, but always in history character have come to people in all sorts of circumstances good or bad, indifferent, when they shouldered their personal responsibilities so repeatedly North wind has made Viking."

In simple words, when needs are full filled easily, without any difficulty with ease, they always expect smooth ride. They cannot think even of little deficiencies and get disturbed, anxious with little blows. When anything adversely happens, they crag to blame others and circumstances and become tense, stressed mentally, because their brains are not trained for blows. But who faced tough times, difficult situation, had courage to face and find ways and means through their ability intelligence and their fighting spirit. they never get disturbed, depressed with small blows in life.

So be bold, accept challenges prepare to face odds, without worrying which lead you to come out of any situation in a best way and will form ladder to reach grate height.

Suppose we are so discouraged that we feel, hopeless, we have two reasons to attempt to turn our Lemons into Lemonade as we have nothing to loose, and every thing to succeed.

a)   We may succeed.

b)   Even if you don't succeed, the mere attempt to turn our minus to plus will cause us to look forward instead of back word.

If you replace negative thoughts with positive one, will release creative energy and spur us to get so busy that we won't have time either for inclination to mown over the past, as past for ever gone.

Hary Emerson Forsdick suggested

1) To have a strong nap and finish out on three strings, that, life is not only life but more than life. It is life is triumphant.

   To cultivate a mental attitude, that will bring us peace and happiness.

Rule :

a) *Where fate hands us lemon, Let's try to make Lemonade.*

b) *Turn your wounds into wisdom.*

c) *Without struggle sucess has no value.*

ಜಜ●ಚಚ

16. How to Cure Depression

Nobody will trouble you or tease you if you take interest in others and see how much you can do them. If you do something to other you will be blessed.

It is clear that if you listen somebody, take interest in their problems, show concern and try to get through from troubles they will definitely bless you. Don't be on the bank and look them, without helping. If you understand other's difficulty and do needful with your suggestion, advise and active help, it will help you in turn in some or other form.

Dr. Frank Loope of Seattle, Washington who was suffering from severe arthritis since 23 years and bed ridden invalid person who get much of his life, who was most unselfish personality has his motto "Itch Dien" it means "I serve". He accumulated address of other invalids and cheered them and himself by writing happy encouraging letters. In fact he organized a letter writing club for invalids and finally formed National Organization called "Shuntin Society".

As he lay in bed, he wrote average 1400 letter a year and brought joy to thousands of invalids by getting Radios and books for Shuntins.

Dr. Loope had the inner glow of a man with purpose a mission. It is the main difference in him and other, joy of knowing that, he was being used by an idea for noble and more significant than himself. Instead of being, as Shaw put in a self centered little cloel of ailment and grievances complaining that the world would not devote itself making him happy.

Baba Amte, Padmashri 1971, Raman Megsaysay 1985, Padma Vibushan 1986 Award Winner from Anandwan Warora, devoted his whole life for leprosy patients at the time there was hue and cry and myth about Leprosy patient they were thrown out of villages and societies as if they were not human being. They use to suffer, but Baba Amte, with his services bring them comfort treated them, trained them for creative profession and thus served them.

Dr. Vikas Amte son of Baba Amte & his wife Dr. Sheetal Amte, through their Lok Biradari Prakalp, Hemalkasa devoted their whole life for the tribal population and provided medical facilities education to the trible, and thus serving the population, what a sacrifice of Amte family.

Dr. Alfred Adler the then psychiatrist to his melancholia patients says, "You can be cured in 14 days if you follow this prescription." Dr. Adler's book "What life should mean to you." Melancholia now regarded as Depression is like a long continued rage and reproach against others though for the purpose of gaining care, sympathy and support. The patient seems only to be dejected about his own guilt.

A Melancholic first memory is generally something like this "I remember, I wanted to lie on bed but my brother was lying there." Melancholic are often inclined to revenge themselves by committing suicide and Doctor first care is to avoid giving them an excuse for suicide, to propose them, "Never do anything, you don't like."

If they are allowed to do what they like; they will not be able to accuse others. It gives satisfaction to his striving for superiority. He is like GOD and can do anything what they like. In fact this does not fit to their lifestyle; as they always want to dominate, accuse others. If you agree with him in all respect, there is no way to dominating them. This rule is great relief and prevents suicide. Generally patient replies, "There is nothing I like doing." Then advise him to refrain from doing anything you dislike. Always agree with him.

The important task imposed by religion has always been

"Love thy neighbour". It is the individual, who is not interested in his fellow men, who has the greatest difficulty in life and provides the greatest injury to others. It is in form of such persons, that all human failure springs.

All that we demand if a human being and highest praised, we can give him is that, he should be a good fellow worker, a friend to all, true partner in love and marriage.

Dr. Adler advised to do a good deed everyday.

A good deed said prophet Mohommad, "Is one that brings smile, joy to the face of other."

While doing good to others, which stop self centered thinking, in turn reduces our worries, fear and depression if at all it is there.

The experience proved necessity of making other happy, in order to be happy our self and our life.

A happiness is contagious, by giving we receive, By helping some one and giving out love, you can win worry and self pity.

Dr. Carl Jung said, "About 1/3 of my patients are suffering from no clinically definable neurosis, but from the senselessness and emptiness, loneliness of their lives, blaming everyone expect themselves and demanding the world should cater to their self centered desires.

By doing something for others, gives greater satisfaction, happiness, calmness and pride to our inner self, which can be felt in our heart, mind and soul.

Aristotle called this attitude as "Enlightened selflessness."

Zoroster said, doing good to other is not a duty it is a joy, it increases your own health and happiness.

Benjamin Fraklin said, "When you are good to other, you are best to yourself."

Thinking of other will not only keep you away from worrying about yourself, it also help you earn lot of friends and have lot of fun and joy. Taking interest in people make beam glow with pleasure.

In Jesus words, "He that findeth his life shall loose it and that looseth his life for my sake find it."

In Bhagwat Gita lord Krishna said, "Believe in me, Have full faith in me and forget your worries. I will take care of every eventuality and care for you.

It means if you care for someone you will be taken care off.

A. E. Housman was an atheist pessimist also felt that, A man who think only of himself would not get much out of his life. He would be miserable but the man who forget himself in service of others, would find joy of living.

Theodore Dresser said, "If a man has to extract any joy out of his life span, he must think and plan to make things better not only for himself but for others, since joy for himself depends upon his joy in others and theirs in him."

Rule :

Forget yourself, Devote for others, A Good, to put smile of joy on someone's face.

Do good for others it will comeback in unexpected way.

The greatest gift, you can give some is your time, your attention, your love, your concern.

Train your mind to see the good, in every situation.

17. Criticism - Be Immune To Criticism

Remember that unjust criticism is often a disguised compliment. Remember that no one kicks the dead dog.

Never be bothered by what people say, as long as you know in your heart, you are right and your purpose, intension is absolutely clear and unselfish.

Do what you feel in your heart to be right.

You will be condemned, if you do so, and damned if you don't. If you get your head above crowd you are going to be criticized. So get used to the idea said by Mathew C. Brugh President International Corporation.

When you in your mind is clear with your idea and if you know that what action you are considering is for betterment of you and your family, without any intension to harm anybody, then go ahead without reconsideration, thinking you will have to face criticism.

So make a Rule.

Do the very best you can, put up your old umbrella, Let the rain of criticism drain off you, instead of rundown by neck.

Deem Taylor went a bit further, he let the rain of criticism rundown the neck and had a laugh, over it in public.

Don't get discouraged with criticism immune your mind of criticism.

Lincon said, "If I were to try to read much less to answer, all the attacks made on me, this shop might as well be closed for any other business. I do the very best, I know how the very best I can, I mean to keep on doing so until end. If end brings me out all right, then what is said against me won't matter. If the end bring me out wrong, the turn angle swearing."

So while taking any thoughtful decision in odd time, be prepared for the worst also and then act on without reconsidering or succumbing to criticism.

If then I was right would make no difference. If I and you are unjustly criticised. Let remember the rule.

Rule :

Do the Best you can, end them up keep open your umbrella, let the rain of criticism run down the back of your neck.

Sometimes just criticism will teach you about your faults which may have been ignored or at all you might have not observed in you, will make you aware of consequences so take it positively if you find it so.

ಐ೮ಐ೮●೮ಽ೮ಽ

18. Self Assessment Introception

Man is never perfect, each and every time. Every body does blunders while making decision. So we should introcept ourselves. Self criticism is very much necessary. As we grow older and wiser to realize our self. In self analysis, we will find nobody is responsible for our own condition, what ever may be good or bad. We only are responsible for our fortune or misfortune.

As human nature tries to blame others for our foolish deeds, misfortunes.

As Nepolean said, "No one but myself, can be blamed for my fate. I have been my greatest enemy, the cause of my own disastrous fate."

H. P. Howell, who was leader of American Finance, Chairman of Board of Commercial National Bank and Trust Company and Director of Several Large Corporations. He grew up with little education and started as clerk in company store. He said, "He used to keep Saturday evening for self examination. This system of self analysis continued for years, had done more for me, than any other thing I have attempted."

Ben Franklin use to do every night self assessment and tried in himself. No wonder he became one of the best loved and most influential personality.

Small man flies and get angry with slightest criticism, but wise man is egar to learn from those, who had censured him and reproved him and disputed the passage with him.

Walt Whitman put it in this way, "Have you learned lesson only of those who admired you and were tender with you and stood aside for you.

Have you not learned grate lesson from those who

rejected you and braced themselves against you and disputed passage with you.

In place of waiting for our enemies to criticize us. Let's be our servere critic. Let's find our remedy for our weakness before other gets chance to criticise and take advantage of it. That's what Charles Darwin did.

Lincon welcome criticism, when he knows it, was sincere, founded on knowledge and given in spirit of help fullness. In marathi there is a proverb. ''निंदकाचे घर असावे शेजारी'' that means, somebody should reside near by us who criticisse us.

So we must welcome that kind of criticism, as we cannot hope to be very right each and every time as human being. Criticism warns us of possible outcome and alert us to reconsider, rethink as well gives us time to correct it timely if he finds scene draw backs in his own procedure and decision.

La Rochefou said, "The opinion of our enemy come nearer to the truth about us than do our own."

If we hear someone has spoken ill of us, Let's not try to defend ourselves. Every fool does so. So Let's be original and humble, acceptable and brilliant.

Let's confound our critic and win applause for ourselves by saying, "If my critic had known about all my faults, he would have criticized me severely.

Hence think about critic, ask yourself, May I deserve this criticism, if I do, I ought to be thankful for it and try to profit by it.

ಐಐ●ಚಚ

19. Fatigue And Worry

Prevention of fatigue leads to prevention of worry Dr. Jacobson, Director of the University of Chicago for clinical psychology declared "Any nervous or emotional state fails to exit in the presence of complete relaxation, that means you cannot worry when you are fully relaxed."

That is fully relaxed body and mind prevents worrying.

So to prevent worry and fatigue Rule is Rest often, Best before you get tired. As our heart to work, to pump blood through the body and keep supplying for whole life, which is expected to 80-100 years ordinarily.

Dr. Walter B. Cannon of Havard Medical School explained it. He said, "Most people have the idea, that heart is working all the time. As a matter of fact, there is a definite rest period at a moderate, normal heart rate 72 / min. The heart is actually working 9 hours out of 24 hours and thus takes rest, total period of 15 hours / day.

Danial W. Jossdyn in his book "Why be tired" observed "Rest is not matter of doing absolutely nothing, but Rest is Repair."

There is so much power in a short period of Rest, that even 5 minutes of nap will help to prevent fatigue.

Edison attributed his enormous energy and endurance to his habit of sleeping whenever he wanted to.

Henry Ford said, "I have never stand up, when I can sit down. I never sit down when I can lie down. So rest is very important part of body energy repair with relaxation.

Horace Mann, "The father of modern education did the same as he grow older, when he was president of Antioch College, he use to stretch out on a coach while interviewing students.

A physical worker, do more work if he is given more time to rest, thus rest can increase workers physical capacity.

Federick Tylor, while as a scientific Management Engineer with the Bethlehem Steel Company. He proved that efficiency can be increased in physical labour if before tired, be given rest period and relaxation at regular intervals.

So take rest before tired and increase efficiency.

20. What Makes You Tired
What Can You Do About It ?

An outstanding fact is "Mental work alone cannot cause fatigue."

Fatigue is scientifically defind as diminished capacity to work. Scientist discovered that blood passing through Brain, when it is active, shows no signs of fatigue at all.

Blood sample collected from working labour and tested, we will find fatigue toxin in the sample.

But Blood sample from Brain of Albert Eianstein will not show fatigue toxins, however at the end of days brain work.

Hence as far as Brain is concern as an organ it can work as well as swiftly at the end of 8 to 12 hours of effort as at the beginning.

Brain is utterly tireless, so what makes you tired.

Psychiatrist declared that most of our fatigue derives from our mental and emotional attitude.

J. A. Hodfield renowned psychiatrist from England in his book, "The Psychological Power" . The greater part of fatigue from which we suffer is of mental origin in fact exhaustion is purely of physical origin.

One American distinguished psychiatrist Dr. A. A. Brill said, "100% of fatigue of sedentary worker in good health is due to psychological factor, by which we mean emotional factors."

What sort of emotional factor tire sedentary workers?

Joy contentment, no, never then what?

Boredom, Resentment feeling of not being appreciated, feeling of futility, hurry, anxiety, worry. These are factors that tire sedentary workers causing fatigue headaches.

We get exhausted, tired because our emotions produce nervous tension in the body, Metropolitan life insurance company pointed out. "Hard work seldom causes fatigue, which cannot be cured by good sleep or rest."

Worry, tension, Emotional upsets are three main causes of fatigue.

Tense muscles are working muscles ease up!

Save energy for important duties, unless our entire body is relaxed, our body at very moment produces nervous tension and muscular strain leading to nervous fatigue.

Why do we produce, these unnecessary tension in doing mental work?

Daniel W. Josselyn says, "I find that chief obstacle is almost universal belief that hard work requires a feeling of effort else it is not well done." When we concentrate we call on our muscles to make the motion of effort, which in no way assist our brain in it's work.

So what is the answer to this nervous fatigue.

That is only one relax, relax and relax. Hence we must know how to relax, while doing our work.

William James said in his essay, "The Gospel of relaxation."

The Americans have over tensions Jerkiness and Breathlessness and intensity agony of expression are bad habits, nothing more or less. Hence Tension is a habit, relaxation is a habit. Bad habits can be broken and good habits can be formed."

How do we Relax?

Do we start with mind?

Do we start with nerves?

Do we start with eighter?

We always begin to relax with muscles. Relaxation to be started with eyes and eye muscles.

Relaxation Technique :-

Close the eyes, lean back and instruct eyes silently, "Let go, Let go." Stop straining, stop frozoning, Let go, Let go. Repeat over and over very slowly.

Eye muscles after few seconds will obey the instructions and relax slowly, then issue command to jaw, facial muscles, neck muscles and thus whole body. In such way Relax the whole body.

Dr. Edmund Jacobson of university of Chicago said, "If you can completely relax your eyes, you can forget all your troubles. The reason is eyes are so important in relaxing nervous tension, that they burn up 1/4 of all the nervous energies, consumed by the body. You can relax in odd moments, almost any where you are. Only don't make efforts to relax, Relaxation is absence of all tension and efforts.

Think ease and relax with closed eyes, suggesting to relax eyes tense muscles gradually relax and slowly issue command to face, neck and thus whole body, it then relax with your command and them feel the energy flowing out of your facial muscles to centre of the body and feel yourself as free from tension as baby.

Yogis in India said, "If you want to learn art of relaxation, observe cat. You will never find tired cat, it is because it become so limp while sleeping.

Once you learn art of relaxation, you will never face insomnia, worry, tensions. Ask yourself, just How tired am I?

If I am tired, it is not because of mental work, I have

done, but because of the way, I have done it.

Daniel W. Josselyn said, "I measure by accomplishment, not by how tired am I, at the end of the day, but at the end of day how tired I am not."

If every businessman in the globe would learn it, our death rate from hypertension, heart attack, strokes will drop significantly. It will reduce hospital load with people who have been broken with fatigue and worries.

Recently new researches showed that two main causes are showing increase of death rate.

a) Lack of sleep

b) Lack of physical exercise

So it is very much necessary to relax in a manner that you abate your worries tensions and prevent toxins due to stress, anxiety etc.

Rule is "Only relax, relax and relax.

The new addiction of screen, i.e. T.V. computers, mobile, laptop always keep your eyes tense, because it is observed that every child from age of 2-3 years to adults and even geriatric population are so addicted to mobile with continuous use of it, even during night when ever wakes up from sleep we use to see mobile, which will in long run prevent you from sleeping peacefully and keep eyes well tense.

This addiction in future will cause so much destruction in human population. It is very powerful addiction as it starts from very early age.

Recently a news was there that a teenage girl aged 15 years committed suicide as she was scolded by parents for excessive use of mobile phone. This is warning sign of vast use of mobile addiction.

There were so many accidents occurred while trying to

capture selfie at picnic spots, tracking paths, while boating in lakes due to drawing while capturing selfie and forgetting they are in mid of lake in boat (Nagpur Tragedy) in which 5 young student lost their life.

While crossing roads many are seen watching and using mobile phones while on two wheelers using mobile. On just for few seconds ot light signal they draw phones and start watching mobiles are now a days becoming killer weapon.

It is observed that parents are using mobiles for baby sitting and they use to say proudly that the babies do not accept feeds without watching screen. They keep T.V. / Mobile in front of child and feed them. Baby does not know taste material what it eats. This is the irony of babies, they even don't know what is apetite.

I have observed many kids in the age group of 4-8 years while screening for yearly medical screening in schools, while working with Address Health Solution, a company from Bengluru in Pune and multiple states.

Number of refractory errors of these kids is quite high and population of student with spectacle is increasing alarmingly.

Screen, mobile addiction is quite dangerous in electro-magnetic waves affecting hearts and brains also.

So it is very much necessary to warn but to whom? It is seen young population is so use to mobile that when they come to home from office, both working couples just get busy with mobiles. They are connected with virtual world, but disconnecting from their own family. Communication between family members with old parents even with the kids is getting affected. Reducing eye contact with family members and ultimately losing love and affection, family bonding, which is very dangerous sign for future. So be alert, think the future of family intimacy getting affected.

We may need large number of de-addiction centres in near future.

ಬ೦ಬ೦●ಙಓಙ

Kid's On The Phone

But so are mamas & papas. There are no easy solutions

A toddler fully engrossed in a smartphone in a noisy public place, her stillness notable against the hubbub, is a common sight today. Indeed, at whatever age a child is introduced to such devices, an intense relationship seems to develop almost by itself. The adults who worry about what copious screen time is doing for children's mental and physical health, do so for good reasons. But the variables are just too fraught for any universal regulation.

In New Zealand a political party has proposed banning the use of mobile phones in schools – "to eliminate unnecessary disturbances and distractions". In India, many schools already have such policies in place. In China government has pushed various apps to limit children to 40 minutes a day plus lock them out from 10 pm to 6 am. It will take time and research to establish that such policies deliver the emotional and cognitive advantages they promise. Meanwhile, there are two broad criticisms here and now. Why blame smartphones for the failure of pedagogy to evolve with technology? Why not address the reasons why children spend so much time on their phones?

Smartphones have even been called 'adult pacifiers'. As much as they cause us anxiety, they also help reduce stress in many contexts. Including as free babysitters when we just don't have the wherewithal for intense parenting. Children won't surrender their screen time before adults do.

21. How To Avoid Fatigue And Keep Looking Young?

In applied psychology to deal with people who are ill from worry, many of these patients emotionally disturbed especially female population.

In 1980 Dr. Joseph H. Pratt observed many patients with physical complaints on careful examination had no signs of physical illness.

He realized that, it was no use to ask patients to go home and forget it. He knew most of the people did not want to be sick. While talking to one lady patient she told, "I use to worry, so much about family trouble, I wished to die, but I learnt at this clinic the futility of worrying."

Dr. Rose Hilferding, the medical adviser of class said that she taught one of the best remedy for lightening worry is "Talking your trouble with someone you trust." We call it "Catharsis". She said, when patient come here, they talk their trouble over at length and breadth until get off their minds. Brooding over worries alone, keep it to oneself causes grate nervous break down. We all have to share worry to whom we trust. Opening up will reduce tension which will help getting relived of our worries. We love to feel, there is some one in the world willing to listen and able to understand us, and have concern to bring out us from worries.

When we open our heart to some, we think will listen us carefully, talk about trouble, we become gradually calm, our mind feels relived of nervous tensions.

What works here?

A little advise, sympathy has actually tremendous healing value. The main motive of counselor is to extract root cause of worry and advice accordingly.

Psychoanalysis is based on to some extent to get facts and root of trouble, once they understand it then healing power of words acts. Analyst have known that a patient could find relief from his inner anxieties if he could talk, open his mind and develop trust in his counselor, just talk how it is because by putting in words, we get better insight into our trouble, get better perspective and think on solving it.

No one knows, but all we know that, "Spitting it out getting it off our chest bring almost instant relief."

Hence "talking things out", then is principle therapies used at Boston Dispensary class.

We can apply this principal at home for trivial domestic problems to solve.

22. How To Banish Boredum, That Produces Fatigue, Worry And Resentment?

It is well known fact that our emotional attitude usually has far more to do with producing fatigue than physical exertion.

Dr. Joseph E Bramach PHD published in Archives of Psychology a report of some of his experiments showing how boredom produces fatigue.

Dr. Bramach put a group of students through a series of tests, which he knew, they would have little interest. The result of students felt tired and sleepy, complaints of headaches, eye strains, felt like irritable.

Medical examination showed

a) Lowered Blood Pressure

b) Reduced oxygen consumption

O2 consumption is reduced - When a person is bored.

But while metabolism picks up immediately as soon as they started to take interest in the task, when given interesting work, and felt pleasure in their work.

We rarely get tired, when we are doing something interesting and exciting pleasurable. If we are interested, excited, exhilarated in some job which gives sense of achievement, we will never tried and fatigued.

It means boredom may tire you in any condition for more than actual strain of work.

Dr. Edward Thordike of Columbia University was conducting experiment on fatigue. He kept young men awake almost 7 days by keeping them constantly interested.

After investigation he reported that boredom is only real

cause of diminished capacity to work called fatigue.

If you are a mental worker, It is seldom, the amount of work you do make you tired, you may be tired by the amount work you do not do.

Our fatigue is not caused by work, but by worry, frustration and resentment.

Captain Andy, captain of the Cotton Bloosm said in one of his philosophical interview "The lucky folks are ones that get to do the things they enjoy doing. Such folks are lucky because they have more energy, more happiness, less worry and less fatigue. Where your interest is there is your energy also.

Walking 10 (ten) blocks with nagging wife or husband can be more tiring than walking 10 (ten) miles with an adoring sweet heart.

Professor Hans Voihinger taught 'as if' we were happy and 'so on'.

If you act 'as if' you are interested in your job, that bit of acting will tend to make interest real. It will also tend to decrease your fatigue, your tension and worries.

If you resolve to make your job, whatever it may be is interesting you will not get bored and fatigued.

As we talk to ourselves with future program, physical exercise, to wake up out of half sleep. But we need even more, some spiritual, mental exercise every morning to stir us into action. Give yourself peptalk every morning.

Is giving yourself of Peptalk every morning silly, superficid childish 'No' is the answer.

On the contrary it is very essence of sound psychology "our life what our thoughts make it". These words are as true today as they were in 18th Century, when Marcus Aurelius wrote them, in his book on meditation.

By talking to oneself, you can direct yourself to think of courage happiness, thoughts of power and peace. By thinking right thoughts, you can make any job less distasteful. Thinking only to getting interested in your job will do much for you. Remind yourself that may be double the amount of happiness you get out of life for which you spent about half of your working hours at your work place.

If you don't find happiness in your job, you may never find it any where. Keep reminding yourself getting interested in your job, will take your mind off your worries and in long run will probably being promotion and pay rise. Even if does not, that will reduce your fatigue to a minimum and help you enjoy your hours of leisure.

So Rule is "Take interest in whatever you do to banish boredom and fatigue."

Four good working habits, that will help to prevent fatigue and worry.

1)   Deal with problem - work on priority fixing in order of their importance.

2)   Solve the problem then and there if you have facts necessary to make decision.

3)   Don't keep putting off decision once made up mind.

4)   Learn to organize, deputize and supervise your own acts.

ಐ೨ಐ೨●ಚಿಚಿ

23. How To Keep Away From Insomnia & Worrying About Sleeplessness?

Samuel Untermyer, a famous Internation lawer who could not get descent sleep in his life. He was worried about his asthma and Insomnia. He could not seem to cure it.

He then decided to do next best thing to take advantage of his wakefulness. Instead of tossing and worrying into a break down, He would get up and study.

The result he began hacking of honour in all his classes and become prodigies of college of city of New York. Even after he started practice law his sleeplessness continued. But he did not worry of it. He said, "Nature will take care of me and Nature did." In spite of small amount of sleep he was getting his health kept up and he was able to work as hard as young Lawers for the New York bar.

He wrote harder he work when they slept. We usually spend 1/3rd of our life in sleeping. Yet nobody knows, what sleep really is?

We know it is a habit and state of rest, in which nature knits up raveled sleeve of care but we don't know how much an individual requires sleep. It may differ person to person and according to age.

Usually new born sleeps 20+ hours as gradually grows sleep time decreases. "Young adult may require 8-9 hours sleep and when grows older if again reduced to 5-6 hours. It is the time to take for repair of wear and tear of days energy losses.

Interesting example, during first world war, Paurlkem a Hungerian Soldger was shot through the frontal lobe, which damaged his sleep center. He could recovered of his injuries, but could not fall sleep. The Biological clock got disturbed.

All sedatives, Narcotics, Hyponotics failed to put him asleep or even to feel drowsy. As per clinicians opinion, he will not live long but he lived in the best of his health for years. He would lie down, close his eyes and took rest but he got no sleep. His case was medical mystery, that upset many of our belief about sleep.

Worry about insomnia will hurt you more than insomnia itself.

Dr. Nathneil Kleitman professor at university of Chicago, had done more research work on sleep. An expert on sleep. He declared that "He had never known any one die from Insomnia. To be sure man might worry about insomnia until he lowered his vitality and it was the worry that did the damage not insomnia itself.

Dr. Kleitman also said, people worry about insomnia usually sleep more than they realize. A man who swears I never slept a minute last night may have slept for hours, without knowing it.

The first requisit for good sound sleep at night is a feeling of security. Dr. Thomas Hislop of great rising asylum stressed that point in an address before British Medical Association. He said, "One of the best sleep producing agent, which my years of practice have revealed to is prayer." I say this purely as Medical Man." Thus he stressed importance of prayer.

The exercise of prayer, in those who habitually exert it must be regarded as the most adequate and normal of all the pacifiers of the mind and calm us of nerves. "Let GOD and Let go."

But if you are not religious by nature and training. Then learn to relax by physical measures.

Dr. David Harold Fink who wrote "Release from

Nervous Tension" say the best way to do this is to talk to your body. Your own suggestion to your eye muscle, face, neck and thus whole body which will act accordingly and go to sleep. Here mental suggestion works.

According to Dr. Fink, words are key to all kinds of Hyponosis, when you are consistently cannot sleep, it is because you are suggesting yourself, thinking of Insomnia and not getting sleep.

The way to undo this is to dehypnotic yourself, and you can do it by saying to your muscle and ultimately to body "Let go, Let go". Loosen up and relax. As we know mind and nerves cannot relax when muscles are tense. If you want to go to sleep and relax, start from eyes muscle to down to rest of body.

The one of the best cure for insomnia is making self physically tired by exhaustive physical work. If you get tired enough nature will force you to sleep, even while you are walking. When we completely exhausted may sleep right through thunder and Horrer.

Dr. Foster Kennedy the famous neurologist told that 5th British Army in 1916 he saw soldiers, so exhausted that they get on the ground, where they were and sleep as sound as coma. They did not even wake up when their eyelids were raised with his fingers. He further said he noticed the pupils of the eye were rolled up.

He said if you roll your eyeballs upward into this position for few minutes you will begin to yawn, and feel sleepy. It is an auto reflex on which we have no control.

ಬಐಬಐ●ಚಚ

24. Happiness

Happiness is not a thing to be traded, no one can buy it nighter can sell it. It cannot be served in plate.

Happiness is a feeling, It is within us. It is a feeling of satisfaction fulfillment, Joy with what you have, where you are and sense of achievement you earned. It is fulfillment of inner desires, which your mind and soul expect from the earthy world. But if you encircle yourself with negative thoughts, unrealistic expectation as castle in air, causing worry, hate, distress, resentment, supreme, selfishness, jealousy, that creates blocks to entry of Happy thoughts to enter your mind and life.

It is very clear that, it only and only you makes yourself happy. You cannot expect it from outside. If you wish to be happy, clear mind blocks you have created and then see magical effects.

Happiness does not depend on what you have, who you are, it solely relies on what you think.

Life is a circle of Happiness, sadness hard times, good times. If you are going through hard times, have faith that good times are on the way.

The art of being happy is to be satisfied with your belonging, which is more than sufficient enjoy it. Don't be greedy to have more and more. It gives just sense of possession and not pleasure and happiness, if you won't utilize it.

Value the time, No body knows about next moment. Hence be happy, make happy, spread love, love music.

I remember a song from old movie, "Baiju Bawara". Music master Haridas, Guru of Tansen, when got bed ridden in his old age with arthritic elements when he heard a song, sung by Baiju.

Hari Om, ''मन तरपत हरी दर्शनको आज''

मन तड़पत हरि दरसन को आज

मोरे तुम बिन बिगड़े सकल काज

आ, विनती करत हूँ, रखियो लाज ।।१।।

तुम्हरे द्वार का मैं हूँ जोगी

हमरी और नजर कब होगी,

सुन मोरे व्याकुल मन की बात ।।२।।

बिन गुरू ज्ञान कहाँ से पाऊँ

दीजो दान हरी गुन गाऊँ, सब गुनी जन पे तुम्हारा राज ।।३।।

मुरली मनोहर आस न तोड़ो, दुख भंजन मोरे साथ न छोड़ो,

मोहे दरसन भिक्षा दे दो आज, दे दो आज ।।४।।

The song and voice, was so effective it sparks his inner instinct, inner energy, he got up from bed, start walking and come down from his hut without support steps down the ladder and takes Darshan of Lord Krishna idol.

Now a days in developed countries, music therapy is being practiced in hospital, during recovery of patients, even doctor, nurses, paramedics fixes timing for music therapy with result of quick recovery and reduce hospital stay and cost.

The creator GOD what you may call supreme power created the world with all diversities to cater essential requirements of all living on this planet in ample, sufficient and more than sufficient to keep living on the planet.

The basic needs of every living kingdom is energy in form of sun, sole source inexhaustibly. Earth planet as base of living. Air /O2 to breathe in ample.

Water for every living, with cycle of utilization and production. Food of different kind in form of plant food, which can be grown on Earth, animal resources, water born species, all sorts are available for consumption and utilization. It is just a cycle born, live and die.

As a matter of fact, life is you are here to live, earn, utilize. No body is allowed to take anything away from here. It is property of supreme creator and he is the only owner of it.

So you came empty handed and will go empty handed, so why to worry. What to worry about. Lastly the message is be happy live happily, cheerfully.

I would like to conclude myself here with a beautiful and meaningful Hindi Bhajan.

25. तोरा मन दर्पण कहलाये

प्राणी अपने प्रभु से पुछे,किस विधी पाऊँ तोहे ।

प्रभु कहे तु मन को पा ले, पा जयेगा मोहे ।

तोरा मन दर्पण कहलाये ।।

भले बुरे सारे कर्मो को देखे और दिखाये ।

तोरा मन दर्पण कहलाये ।।

मन ही देवता, मन ही ईश्वर, मन से बड़ा न कोय ।

मन उजीयारा जब जब फैले, जब उजीयारा होय।

इस उजले दर्पण पे प्राणी, धूल न जमने पाये ।

तोरा मन दर्पण कहलाये ।

सुख की कलियाँ, दुख के कांटे मन सबका आधार ।

मन से कोई बात छुपे ना मन के नैन हजार ।

जग से चाहे भाग ले कोई, मन से भाग न पाये ।

तोरा मन पर्दण कहलाये ।

तन की दौलत, ढलती छाया मन का धन अनमोल ।

तन के कारण, मन के धन को मन माटी मेइन रौंद ।

मन की कदर भुलानेवाला वीराँ जनम गवाये।

तोरा मन दर्पण कहलाये ।

26. स्वर्गीय लता मंगेशकर के आखरी शब्द

उन्होने लिखा,

इस दुनियाँ में मौत से बढ़कर, कोई सच नही । दुनियाँ की सबसे मेहंगी ब्रँडेड कार, मेरे घर पे खड़ी है । लेकीन मुझे व्हील चेअरपर बिठा दिया गया । मेरे पास इस दुनियामें, हर तरह के डिझाईन और रंग के मेहंगे कपडे, मेहंगे जुते, मेहंगे सामान है । लेकीन मैं छोटे गाऊन में हूँ । ज्यो मुझे अस्पताल ने दिया । मेरे बँक खाते में बहुत पैसा है, लेकीन यह मेरे किसी कामका नही । मेरा घर मेरे लिए महल जैसा है, लेकीन मैं अस्पताल में एक छोटे से बिस्तर पर लेटी हूँ । मैं दुनियाँ के पाँच सितारा होटलों में घुमती रही । अब मुझे अस्पताल के एक प्रयोगशाला से दुसरी प्रयोगशाला में भेजा जा रहा है । एक समय था, जब हर दिन ७ हेअर स्टाईलिस्ट मेरे बालों की सफाई करते थे । लेकीन आज मेरे सिरपर बाल नहीं है । मैं दुनियाँ भरके, विभीन्न फाईव्ह स्टार होटलों में खाना खाती थी । पर आज तो दिन में दो गोली, और रात में एक बुंद नमक मेरा आहार है । मैं विभीन्न विमानोपर, दुनियाँ भर में यात्रा कर रही थी । लेकीन आज दो लोग अस्पताल के बरामदें में जाने में मेरी मदद कर रहे है । किसीभी सुविधाने, मेरी मदद नही की । किसी तरह आराम नही । लेकीन कुछ अपनों के चहरे, उनकी दुवाएँ, मुझे जिंदा रखती है । आप खाली हाथ ही निकलेंगे । दयालु बनो, उनकी मदद करो जो कर सकते हो । पैसा और पावर वाले लोगों को अहमीयत देने से बचे । अपने लोगो से प्यार करो । भले वह आपके लिए, भला बुरा कहे । पर आप उनकी सराहना करे । कि वे आपके लिए क्या है? उनका सपोर्ट करो, उनके दु:ख दर्द में शामील हो ।